GOLF:
THE TECHNIQUE
BARRIER

GOLF:
THE TECHNIQUE
BARRIER

by

MINDY BLAKE
D.S.O., D.F.C., M.Sc.

SOUVENIR PRESS

Contents

5

'You have given me new hope'

IN 1972, I helped Mindy Blake to write a book called *The Golf Swing Of The Future*, which suggested that there was a better way of hitting a golf ball than the world had yet tried. Briefly, his theory was this. Golf like field athletics, is a technical sport. In field athletics, development of a scientific technique has led to dramatic increases in the distances which man can throw a javelin, discus or shot. If the same technique were applied to golf—and he outlined how he thought this could be done—it would result in an equally dramatic improvement in performances on the golf course.

He was, in fact, looking forward to golf's equivalent of the four-minute mile, but his theory was not aimed solely at enabling the best golfers to play even better than they do already. He made the point: 'If one compares golf to the piano, I should say that being able to play golf at the level of a Nicklaus or Palmer involves at least as much effort as is needed to turn yourself into a concert pianist. Probably it needs even more. To strike a more optimistic note, however, to be able to play to a handicap of 10 is no more difficult than being able to give a reasonable rendition of *Chopsticks*.' Once a golfer had reached this standard further progress was purely a matter of dedication and practice. The proviso, of course, was that you should be building on the sound technique he advocated.

Everyone agreed that it was difficult to fault *The Golf Swing Of The Future* in terms of logic and the book received generous reviews. The consequences were interesting. Predictably, the golfing establishment tended to retire to the nearest bunker and hide its head in the sand. At the same time, a heated controversy, which has not entirely subsided even now, five years later, broke out in the columns of the magazine *Golf World*. But the most significant reaction came from ordinary golfers.

They tracked Mindy down to his home at Wentworth and bombarded him with letters, and frequently with telephone calls, from various parts of Britain, Ireland, Australia, New Zealand, South Africa, France, Germany, Switzerland and Scandinavia. Nearly all of them had the same complaint: they had read all the books and tried all the pros. but their golf wasn't getting any better and, in the majority of cases, it was getting worse. His ideas, they said, made sense, but before trying to put them into practice they wanted to check on a variety of points so that they could be sure they were working on the right lines.

After the letters and telephone calls came the pilgrims, who wanted to see things with their own eyes. They included a golfer who made a round trip of nearly 300 miles from the Midlands every Friday afternoon, over a period of several months, in order to spend half an hour or so hitting balls under Mindy's critical eye. Others flew over from the Continent, and the whole process was accelerated the following year when *The Golf Swing Of The Future* appeared in the United States and the American publishers said: 'Come on over for a month and bring your golf clubs.'

During his four weeks on the other side of the Atlantic, the places he visited included Boston, Harford, New York, Philadelphia, Washington, West Virginia, Houston, Los Angeles, San Francisco and Chicago. He appeared on 25 local TV shows and one coast-to-coast programme, and he was also a guest on three or four radio shows daily wherever he stopped. In addition, he played several rounds of golf and gave a number of demonstrations.

Of his performances as a golfer during the visit, he says that he 'played rather badly.' This modest assessment needs to be put into some kind of perspective which takes into account the constant travelling, the strain of undergoing a public examination of his method, and the fact that, even if he returned a 68 on a strange course, he would be inclined to say he had 'played quite well and been a bit lucky.' The following is a newspaper account of a demonstration he gave at Long Island:

'I have seen the golf swing of the future—and it works. At least, it works as executed by Mindy Blake, a 5ft. 8in., 151-pound, bespectacled 60-year-old who hits (nay, drags) golf shots that fly (nay, float) up to 280 yards, straight as an arrow. That's with the small English ball. But Mindy drives the American ball 230 to 240 yards, just as straight. Straight is the operative word in Mindy's golf vocabulary. Although the distance he gets is impressive for a man of his age and modest, if wiry, physique, distance is not his primary concern. His objective is what he calls "accuracy of length"—playing every shot to a spot, regardless of distance—and he achieves it with remarkable consistency.

'In a recent practice session on Long Island, I watched Mindy loft a dozen beat-up American golf balls with an 8-iron. Ten of his shots ended up in a neat little row, 140 yards away. You almost literally could have covered the ten with a bushel basket. The other two shots were "poor" by Mindy's standards in that they landed about five yards past the bunched ten.

'Mindy's practice drives went well over 200 yards, and he was obviously not at his best when I watched him drive. Mindy is no cool pro.—he appears to be somewhat self-conscious and nervous about his sudden celebrity as a golf author and ground-breaking stylist. I asked him to match drives with Gene Francis, a long-hitting, tournament calibre Long Island amateur, and Mindy was plainly tense and ill-at-ease. He got off some dubbed shots. He also got off several good ones, not as long as Francis's 260-yard boomers, but Mindy didn't disgrace himself. And, after a while, all his drives were landing close to the same spot . . .'

A few days later, while in Richmond, Virginia, he was invited to play some golf with Mrs. Donald O'Brien, six times the city champion, at the James River course of the Country Club of Virginia. At the 160-yard 17th he took a 6-iron from the tee and holed out in one. He was, he says, again playing 'rather badly' and the ace was 'a fluke,' but a hole in one is still not exactly a bad advertisement if you are saying: 'I think this is the best way to hit a golf ball.'

In conversation and argument with a number of American pros., he found them extremely open-minded. 'In general,' he says, 'they felt instinctively that there was a more effective way of hitting a golf ball than they had yet discovered. But their main interest was to see whether I had found anything which they could adapt to their own individual swings.' Once again, however, the main appeal was to the ordinary club golfer.

His return home was followed by a cascade of letters from various parts of the United States. Wrote one golfer from Massachusetts: 'I love the game, but I was thinking of giving it up. I have been working at it for years without any real improvement. The ideas you put forward make so much sense that you have given me new hope.' As in the case of many European correspondents, this writer asked for clarification of certain points to ensure he would be working on the correct lines when he started to try to master the new swing.

The letters from America, like the letters from various parts of Europe, were followed by the pilgrims. Several millionaires flew the Atlantic solely for the purpose of spending a few hours talking to Mindy, watching him and trying to emulate him. Others, who had already planned a European vacation, altered their schedule so that they could drop in at Wentworth. He also received a number of requests for a home movie of his method.

Today, nearly five years later, Mindy has a file of several hundred letters from all over the world, almost unanimous in their gratitude to him because his book fulfilled its promise and opened the path to better golf. The following is a brief selection. We have taken the view that the state of a man's swing, like the state of his heart, lungs and liver, should be discussed with a certain measure of reticence. With this in mind, we have given the place of origin of the letters, but not the names of the writers:

'I don't know that I told you how I decided to try your method, but it might be of interest to you. I was intrigued by the title, bought the book, and was part way through reading it when it suddenly occurred to me that someone I play with occasionally was doing the things you advocate. I called him next morning and found that he had indeed read your book early in the summer and had been using your swing. The interesting part about it is that he is playing better than ever before and with great consistency. His handicap had gone from 15 to 10 and he was breaking 80 occasionally . . .'

NEW HAVEN, Connecticut.

'At the beginning of 1973, I had decided to give up golf when I saw a review of your book *The Golf Swing Of The Future*. I ordered the book and, for the first time in my golfing life, spanning approximately 41 years, I felt I was reading a book on golf which was both logical and definite. Needless to say I have read the majority of the books published on golf during the last 40 years, but none has impressed me at all, as each one offered a different approach.

'I am now 69 years of age, but when I was much younger, especially during a six-month visit to the golf courses of Scotland and England in 1951, I was playing down to a 3 handicap. With the passing of the years, however, the usual creeping-on of old age created a less-supple framework with a resultant loss of distance and a chronic built-in slice. I have always had a slight fade in my game, but the last decade has produced a slice which all my efforts failed to eradicate . . .

'When I received your book, I decided to give the game a last fling. For approximately a year I battled away, not every day but about two or three times a week. The first attempts were completely disastrous, but I was convinced that your logical approach was the correct one. Gradually my game began to build up again, and, joy of joys, I had some terrific hooks and draws. If anything was needed to buck me up, this feature in my swing convinced me that I was progressing on the right lines.

'I will not bore you with further background details, but I wanted you to get the picture of my resuscitated passion for the game. Today I have a handicap of 11, and, if the putts drop, this can easily be around 8. I generally play to a stroke or two of my handicap either way, whereas before I was usually miles above the 14 then allotted to me. My drives are generally long and *straight*, and at times I appear to be able to draw at will. My irons need a lot of work, but these factors are minor to the pleasure I am again getting out of the game . . .'

PRETORIA, S. Africa.

'I wish to thank you for publishing *The Golf Swing Of The Future*. I know it off by heart, and since applying your technique I hit the ball much further. The margin of error is now so little and every ball goes down the middle. It is less tiring and I can manage 18 holes quite well as less effort is needed. Considering I am 80 years old next February, I have a lot to be thankful for.'

SUTTON COLDFIELD, England.

'I am happy to relate that everything has finally fallen into place. I got a bigger thrill yesterday when I went to the practice ground than at any time in all the years I have played golf. As a matter of fact, I didn't want to go home—for fear I'd lose the touch, I guess. My major complaint has been that I was unable to get any distance with my clubs and that is when I started to pursue your method.

'You were absolutely right when you said that there would be highs and lows. I struggled for ten months, and I am glad I stayed with it because yesterday it all came together. I was driving the ball further than ever before and with much less effort. I was relaxed, I had more freedom of movement and my grip was correct, and when I hit a 7-iron 150 yards, I knew something right had happened . . . Before the summer is out I will send you a few of my scores, and, for a guy of 70, I think that I am going to surprise you . . .'

GLENDALE, California.

'At the age of 71, I am hitting the ball more consistently, further and better than ever before—thanks to you and my persistence to stick it out and see it through. I am enjoying myself on the golf course more than at any time I can remember. I have disproved the theory that age was the reason for losing distance . . . Finally, after many months of practice, I am able to keep the ball in play down the middle. No more banana balls, and an occasional pull to the left, but not too often. It is a whole new ball game . . .'

Same correspondent, 11 months later.

'When I wrote to you last month, I said I would give you another progress report on my golfing at the end of the summer. Well, Mindy, I cannot wait until the end of the summer because so much has happened. I am sending you a score card from the golf course where I play. It is a public course where they are at present conducting the Los Angeles City Championships . . . Today was the highlight for me when I finished with an 84. I am confident now that I can break 80.

'. . . I was able to get 18 very good tee-shots. That has never happened to me before. I was able to keep the ball down the middle on every hole. I avoided all the sand traps and was not out of bounds . . . On the 15th hole, which is a par 3, 170 yards, I was on the pin all the way, against the wind, and the ball stopped just two feet from the flag. With a bit of luck, it might have been a hole in one. The putt was straight in for a birdie and was I ever thrilled.

'I have you to thank for a fine method. I am glad I had the courage to try and the persistence to stay with it. I am also happy to say that I would not be embarrassed to play with anyone now, even Jack Nicklaus.'

Same correspondent, one month later.

'I have just recently bought a copy of your book *The Golf Swing Of The Future*, and have proved it to be the most interesting book on the golf swing I have read since Hogan's *Modern Fundamentals* and *Lessons With Mr. X*. You have taken over where they left off, and to my mind it could prove the greatest advance since the change to the rubber-cored ball.

'I play to 15 at present but am too inconsistent. As a result of business pressure, I can play only two out of three weekends. Nevertheless, I generally average between six and eight pars, but I come to grief on relatively easy holes, usually the par 3s, because of *lack of direction*. This is my greatest fault. I average 230 yards off the tee and do not always find the fairway.

'I have used your method for a week and, as stated in the book, realize I shall have to apply myself diligently to single figures. Nevertheless, having been to the driving range three times in the last week, I have already found that I am driving straighter . . .'

CASTLECOVE, New South Wales.

'I have incorporated your swing into mine. When properly hit, my shots go down the middle with added distance and a good flight. After six months, the good hits work out at about 40 to 60 per cent. each round. I am also saving shots with my approaches to the green.'

HAMMOND, Indiana.

'I want to thank yoù for giving, for the first time, direction to someone who, like you, has been a gymnast and an athlete and, above all, a golf enthusiast. But, unlike you, I managed by a keen study of all the swing methods to increase my handicap from single figures to double figures. Your book does indicate to me the finally correct direction for all of us to go—so, many thanks!'

MOFFAT, Dumfriesshire.

'About a year before I found your book, I had a severe case of the shanks, which included days when I shanked every iron shot undertaken. The pro. watched me shank and said: "There are eight ways to shank and you are guilty of all nine." With the shank, my handicap went from 11 to 15 and it should have been 20. Then, with the aid of your book, I went from 15 down to 9 with several rounds in the high 70s and always under 85. This included breaking par for nine holes three times, which is indeed rare for this chopper.

'I enjoyed all aspects of the book, and, when word got around about a 34 on the back nine East, I had to get six copies and set up a library in the upper locker. The assistant pros. were aghast, but the assistant pros. are flat-bellied with hip turns of 405 degrees. The writer, at 56, is anything but flat, with the fastest backswing in the West . . .'

NEW YORK, N.Y.

Nearly every one of the writers quoted above asked for various points in the book to be clarified or amplified. In all, Mindy has had to answer at least 10,000 queries by letter, on the telephone and in conversation with pilgrims to his home in the last five years. At the moment of writing, one group of a dozen Canadian golfers is planning a charter trip to Britain because they cannot agree on their interpretation of Mindy's swing. This evidence suggests certain deficiencies in *The Golf Swing Of The Future*. It is never, of course, easy to learn a physical movement from the printed page. Nevertheless, many correspondents felt the task would not be beyond them 'if only you would write a much more detailed book about your ideas and, in particular, a book with more precise illustrations.'

The intervening years have also made it clear that *The Golf Swing Of The Future* did not place enough emphasis on the fact that it was describing an integrated swing. Certain of its basic principles would improve any swing, but after that point you had to go the whole hog if you wished to achieve success.

For example, one of Mindy's fundamental, and quite accurate, tenets is that most bad golf stems initially from bad posture. He wrote: 'Actually, I doubt whether more than five amateur golfers in a hundred, at any level of the game, have a sound posture. The contortions of most Sunday morning swings are the result of trying to compensate for bad posture, and so are the majority of quick hooks, wild slices and raised heads. Posture is the foundation of the swing and, if your golf goes off, nine times out of ten the cause will be bad posture.'

The worst fault of all, he said, was having a bad hip-shoulder relationship at the address. The shoulders *must* be square to the line of flight and the hips *must* be slightly more open. Otherwise, the hips would collapse (that is, turn with the shoulders) on the backswing and there was no way back to the ball without yanking down with the hands and arms.

With any swing, he went on, a correct hip-shoulder relationship could be achieved at the address by having the shoulders square and turning both feet towards the hole, the left foot 30 degrees, the right foot 10 degrees. This opened the hips in relation to the shoulders. Turning the right foot also inhibited the action of the flexible ball-joint in the right hips and prevented the hips from turning with the shoulders on the backswing.

This was an easy-enough concept to put over and an easy-enough concept to grasp. Nearly everyone who tried this hip-shoulder relationship found immediately, they said, that they hit the ball better than ever before in their lives. Many decided that was sufficient progress. Others, encouraged, pushed on to other aspects of the swing. It was then that problems began to emerge.

When it was possible to analyse complaints about lack of progress, the cause was almost always the fact that a golfer had overlooked some part of the swing or dismissed it as unimportant. The following letter from Barstow, California, summarises the situation neatly:

'I knew your swing was sound! I worked at everything you said in your letters, but something was still wrong. It felt tight. No distance. So I went through your book again. It was very simple. You kept telling us over and over again, even as a final word in the last paragraph, always to be certain that your eyes are in a vertical plane (i.e. one above the other).

'Well, that was it! I had gradually raised by eyes, so my swing was, or wanted to go, flat or horizontal. I played a few holes last night and the change was something to behold. My driver is being repaired and I used a 4-wood. The distance off the tee was further than my previous drives. The accuracy improved also. No tightness. I'm on the right track. What a feeling of confidence!

'I'll keep you posted, but I'm a little closer to that game in the low 70s than when I first read your book.

I don't know how you ever worked out all the many little important details of the swing, but I'm very grateful. Tell others! There is *no* mixing your swing with any other method. Dilute it and the results are diluted . . .'

In the light of all this experience, it seemed a good idea to produce a book which would amplify and clarify the swing described in *The Golf Swing Of The Future*, and emphasise the importance of the points which tended to be overlooked. Then something else emerged. One of the main objections Mindy encountered in discussing his method with pros. was that they felt only a very supple person could perform one of the movements he recommended—a full shoulder turn without turning the hips.

He found this criticism rather puzzling because he is not, he says, a particularly supple person himself. Furthermore, the age of many of the golfers who achieved successful results with his swing suggested that they, too, were unlikely to be very supple. After a good deal of reflection, and observation of golfers trying to use this method, it became clear that he had been dealing with a non-argument.

It *is* the case that you have to be supple to combine his swing with the shoulder turns which accompany the early Scottish swing and the modern square-to-square swing. However, without realising it, he had stumbled upon a third, and radically different, type of shoulder turn, which rendered the arguments about suppleness no longer relevant.

Once he had grasped this point, it was also evident to him that his ideas on posture, while fundamentally correct, had not been carried to their logical conclusion. When they were carried to their logical conclusion, it became very much easier to explain his ideas and to execute the swing which he believes will be accepted one day as the only sound method from an athletic and scientific point of view of hitting a golf ball.

This book is therefore not just a more detailed account of his method, but an extension of his method. For me, it has again been a pleasure to help in putting these ideas on paper and—as we both hope—making a contribution to a deeper understanding of the most fascinating, and most difficult, of all ball games.

HARRY WEAVER

About This Book

EVEN the best players do not play very good golf most of the time and the standard of ordinary club golfers is relatively poor. Nor are either the best players or ordinary club golfers consistent. They are prone to play miles above themselves one day and miles below themselves the next. Why should this be?

I have tried to explain the reason in this book by tracing the evolution, such as it has been, of the golf swing, and demonstrating that golf is face to face with a technique barrier which inhibits any advance in the game's standards. I have also shown how this barrier can be pierced and described what I believe to be the ultimate form of the golf swing—a swing which should enable anyone, no matter what their present standard, to play better and more consistent golf.

There is not much point in saying that you have found what you believe to be the ultimate form of the golf swing and then not giving sufficient details to enable interested golfers to try it out. I should like to make it clear, however, that this book is meant to be a contribution to the theory of golf, not an instruction manual.

Mindy Blake,
Wentworth, 1977.

1: The Wasted Years

IF you examine results in any sport where performance can be measured, two points emerge very clearly. In the first place, there is a steady, and sometimes dramatic, improvement over the years. Secondly, today's sensation quickly becomes the norm and is soon forgotten as athletes of various types press on to set new standards of speed, height and distance. The world's first sub-four minute mile by Roger Bannister in 1954 is a case in point. It was hailed, quite rightly, as an heroic sporting achievement. But today any first-class field is peppered with athletes who have run the distance in less than four minutes, and, at the time of writing, the world record is held by Walker of New Zealand with a time of 3min. 49.4sec.

This pattern of progress—particularly striking in field athletics, which bear direct comparison with golf in the sense that all are purely technical sports—has not been repeated on the golf course. It is, of course, difficult to assess this matter with absolute precision because of the changes which have taken place in golf equipment, and in the length and quality of courses, over the last century or so.

The first major change in the golf ball came about 1848 when 'featheries,' made of leather and stuffed with sufficient feathers to fill a top hat, gave way to 'gutties,' made from gutta percha, which was employed initially as protective packing for goods

23

shipped to Britain from India. The advantages of 'gutties' were considered to be cheapness, standardisation of shape, durability and accuracy rather than a great increase in distance, and it was to be half a century before they were replaced by the rubber-cored ball, invented by Dr. Coburn Haskell, an American.

Dr. Haskell's forerunner of the modern ball had a stormy introduction. His patent was opposed on the grounds that all the materials used in the ball had been employed previously for other purposes, and, once that obstacle had been overcome, the ball was found to burst rather readily and to be excessively lively on the green. Nevertheless, it gave much greater distance and its future was assured when Alex 'Sandy' Herd favoured the new ball in winning the 1902 British Open while the great triumvirate—John H. Taylor, Harry Vardon and James Braid—stuck to 'gutties.' Herd's score of 307, which beat Vardon by one stroke and was more than seven strokes better than the average total for the previous ten British Opens, was sufficient to relegate 'gutties' to the museum. Although courses were gradually lengthened to compensate for the new ball, average scores in the British Open over the next quarter of a century dropped to just over 75 compared with 78.5 in the years 1892–1901.

With the actual clubs used, the really significant development, in terms of distance and control, was the legalizing of steel shafts in the United States in 1926 and in Britain in 1929. Courses were again lengthened and generally made more difficult to compensate for the increased power provided by steel shafts.

From the point of view of accuracy, modern golfers also enjoy several other advantages over players in the past. Strains of grass have been developed which restrain a ball from scuttling along for yards, and possibly into trouble, after landing. Greens are manicured and well-watered. If a golfer does get into trouble, he can call on that great saviour, the wedge.

It is thought that the original sand-wedge—a hickory-shafted club, which weighed 23 ounces against the 13 ounces of the average club and had a concave face and rounded sole—was invented in the mid-1920s by a Texas cotton broker named Edwin McClaine, who had his invention made up for him by a blacksmith. The story goes that Bobby Jones heard about the club, ordered one from the same blacksmith, and used it in the process of winning his Grand Slam in 1926.

Nevertheless, the credit for inventing the sand-wedge as we know it today is normally given to Gene Sarazen, who wrote in an American magazine a couple of years ago: 'The wedge is a variation of the sand-iron I designed (back at the beginning of the 1930s) by adding solder to the back of a niblick. I was taking flying lessons at the time. I noticed when I pulled the stick the tail would lower and the plane would take off. It occurred to me that, if I put a tail on a niblick, I could get the ball up and out of the sand easier. I tried it and it worked.

'I didn't tell anyone about my discovery. I took the club with me to the British Open in 1932 and kept it hidden. When I showed during the first few holes that the club invariably could get me out of the sand and close enough to the hole to get down in one putt, everyone began talking about it. I won that championship by five strokes . . . and manufacturers started putting out sand irons by the thousand.' In fact, Sam Snead says of the wedge: 'This club is the principal reason why scoring generally has been lowered so fantastically since the Bobby Jones era, even though the courses on the whole are longer and tougher.'

To sum up this brief dissertation on equipment and courses, the tournament golfer today, compared with the tournament golfer of a century or more ago, enjoys the benefit of high-compression, long-flying golf balls, powerful steel-shafted clubs, fairway grass designed to 'hold' a ball, and immaculate, true-running greens. As a counterbalance, he is faced by longer and tougher courses. The evidence suggests, however, that making courses longer and more difficult has been a relatively unimportant factor, and the modern pro. should find golf a very much easier game than did his counterpart in the middle of the 19th century.

In his book *Never On Weekdays*, that most entertaining of golf writers, Henry Longhurst, compares the task faced by Willie Auchterlonie when he won the British Open on the Old Course at St. Andrews in 1893, and that faced by Arnold Palmer in his historic British Open victory at Troon in 1962:

'Over the Old Course, which then measured 6,487 yards, Auchterlonie had to take a wooden club for his second at no fewer than 12 holes. There were six which he could not reach in two, and at two of these he had to take the equivalent of a 4-iron for his third. At Troon, on the other hand, which we may take to have measured a minimum of 7,000 yards, Palmer reached five greens with a drive and the smallest club in the bag, the wedge, and six more with anything from a 6-iron down to a 9. Of the two very long holes, he reached one with a 3-wood (for his second shot) and the other with a 1-iron and a very short chip. So, while Auchterlonie took a wooden club for his second shot 12 times, Palmer needed nothing more than a 6-iron to a wedge 11 times.'

In the light of this it is interesting to examine the score returned by Tom Morris, Jnr., then aged 19, when he won the third of his four successive British Open titles at Prestwick in 1870. The championship consisted at that time of three 12-hole rounds. In his valuable *Encyclopaedia Of Golf*, Nevin H. Gibson gives the following analysis of the champion's performance, adjusting the modern concept of par to make allowance for the fact that Morris was using wooden-shafted clubs and the 'guttie' ball, and was therefore at a disadvantage over distance. It has also to be borne in mind that he was putting on greens which were worse than the majority of fairways on which golf is played today.

No.	Name	Length	Par	1st	2nd	3rd
1.	Start	578 yards	5	3	5	5
2.	Alps	385 yards	5	5	5	5
3.	Tunnel Out	167 yards	3	3	2	3
4.	Stone Dike	448 yards	5	5	5	7
5.	Sea He'therick	440 yards	5	6	6	4
6.	Tunnel In	314 yards	4	3	5	5
7.	Green Hollow	144 yards	3	3	3	3
8.	Station	166 yards	3	3	4	3
9.	Burn	395 yards	5	4	5	5
10.	Sauch House	213 yards	4	3	3	4
11.	Short Hole	132 yards	3	4	4	3
12.	Home Hole	417 yards	4	5	5	4
TOTAL		3,799 yards	49	47	51	51

This adds up to one eagle (on the 578-yard opening hole, a remarkable achievement which must have put him in good spirits for the rest of the tournament), six birdies, 20 pars, eight bogeys and one double-bogey. The reduction of the accepted lengths of par to give Morris an allowance of four strokes a round does not

seem over-generous in view of Henry Longhurst's
Auchterlonie–Palmer comparison or the result of an
interesting match played at Westward Ho! in 1974
when the British club celebrated its centenary.

On one side were the Moderns (Peter Alliss, Brian
Huggett), on the other the Ancients (Max Faulkner,
Christy O'Connor). Messrs. Faulkner and O'Connor
wore the red coats and drainpipe trousers affected by
golfers in the 1860s, used the 'guttie' and were
equipped with a selection of century-old clubs with
wooden shafts and pig-iron heads. In a try-out before
the actual match, the local pro. found at one hole that
he could not carry a bunker 170 yards distant. At the
551-yard 17th, while his assistant was on the green
with a drive, 3-wood and 9-iron, he found himself in
a ditch 40 yards short after three full shots. As a
matter of interest, the Ancients, who received 12 shots
(one at each par 4 and par 5 hole), won by one hole,
but only after O'Connor had sunk a 40-yard approach
with a rusty, sharp-faced niblick to halve the 18th.

Making allowances for the equipment he played
with and the condition of courses at that time,
Morris's score of two over par compares very favour-
ably with performances more than a century later and
would, in fact, put him among the money in a present-
day tournament. The implication is that better
equipment and truer courses have been the major
influences in improving golf standards while golfers—
or, to be more precise, the technique of golfers—has
played only a very minor role.

To rely too much on the case of Tom Morris would,
of course, be somewhat fanciful as we are basically
comparing like with unlike. There is, however, plenty
of evidence in more modern times to support the
argument that golf lacks any pattern of steady progress, or the ability to build upon what has been

shown to be possible. The exceptional round is not regarded, as it would be in comparable sports, as the target to be aimed at, and improved upon, if a pro. is to remain at the top. Rather is it looked upon as what the insurance companies describe as 'an act of God.' It is something mystical and, as such, can be explained only in mystical terms. 'Inspired' is the adjective most commonly used, with the inspiration coming from some ill-defined interior source or from the mysterious 'Fates', who chose this particular day to smile upon one particular golfer and ensure that everything went right for him. Once the commotion has subsided, the brilliant achievement passes into the folklore of golf and into the record books, and it is usually disinterred only some years, or even some decades, later in stories which begin: 'Not since . . .'

For example, Tom McNamara had a 69 (as well as a 77) when he finished runner-up in the U.S. Open in 1909, and a 69 (plus an 80) when he finished in the same position in 1912. Walter Hagen had a record-tying 68 in the opening round when he won his first title in 1914. It had therefore been demonstrated before the start of the first World War that there was nothing sacrosanct about either par or the figure 70. Yet it was not until 1930 that Bobby Jones (71,73,68, 75) became the first golfer to win the U.S. Open with a total below par.

I think it is fair to say that, in any comparable sport, it would not have been long after this barrier had been breached before somebody did the equivalent of breaking par in all four rounds. The U.S. Open had to wait 38 years. Lee Trevino was the first player to perform this feat when he returned 69,68,69,69— against par of 70—to win the championship at Rochester, N.Y., in 1968. Up to the time of writing, Tony Jacklin is the only player to repeat the achievement with rounds of 70,71,70,70 against a par of 72 to take the title at Chaska, Minnesota, in 1970.

Even now, nearly half a century after Bobby Jones showed that it was possible, it is unusual for a winner of the U.S. Open to return a total below par. Over the last dozen championships, only 18 players have managed it, and nine of those did so in the same year. The details are: 1965, none; 1966, two; 1967, two; 1968, two (including Lee Trevino); 1969, none; 1970, one (Tony Jacklin); 1971, none; 1972, none; 1973, nine (this was the year Johnny Miller headed the field, adding a remarkable last-day 63 to his previous 71,69,76); 1974, none; 1975, none; 1976, three.

In assessing these results, some allowance has to be made for the relative difficulty of the courses and the weather conditions when the tournament was played. When Hale Irwin won at Winged Foot, N.Y., in 1974 with a score of 287 (73,70,71,73), seven over par, one writer described the course as '6,961 yards of agony with tight fairways, heavy rough, a multitude of intrusive trees, nearly three acres of bunker sand and small rolling greens.' Nevertheless, the course was not beyond taming. Par was equalled in the first round and scores of 69, one under, returned in each of the other three rounds.

Similarly, when Jack Nicklaus won at Pebble Beach, California, in 1972 with rounds of 71,73,72,74 for a total of 290, two over par, heavy rough and slick greens were said to have made life difficult for the players and a strong wind ensured 'an appalling last day.' Yet, once again, somebody managed to improve on par of 72 in every round, the best scores each day being 71,68,71,70.

Oddly enough, despite complaints about un- predictable bounces and strong winds, the world's leading pros. have tended to perform rather better on the seaside links where the British Open is played. The figures for sub-par rounds over the last dozen years are: 1965, nine; 1966, three; 1967, 12; 1968, none; 1969, four; 1970, seven; 1971, 24; 1972, five; 1973, six; 1974, one; 1975, 15; 1976, four. Three winners in this period—Roberto de Vincenzo (1967), Lee Trevino (1971) and Tom Weiskopf (1973)—have managed to improve on par and this achievement was matched by Jack Nicklaus when he came second in 1967 and by six of the runners-up in 1971.

Although better than the U.S. figures, these totals are not really remarkable when set against the hundreds of golfers who have taken part in the last 12 championships, and, whether in the British Open or other tournaments, it is rare for the world's best players to repeat what has been shown to be possible in the past. Henry Cotton had rounds of 67,65,72,79 when he won the British Open for the first time in 1934. Today, 43 years later, 79s remain more common than 65s. In fact, despite the thousands of rounds played, only seven players have since managed to equal his 65 and only 18 have managed to equal the 66 he returned when winning the title for the second time in 1948.

There have been some even more remarkable scores for nine holes and for full rounds in the qualifying stages of the tournament. In the Open itself, Tom Haliburton and Peter Thomson (1963) and Tony Jacklin (1973) have recorded outward halves of 29, and eight players have had scores of 30 for nine holes, Four—Frank Jowle (1955), Peter Thomson (1958). Maurice Bembridge (1967) and Malcolm Gunn (1972)—have come into the clubhouse with scores of 63 while qualifying.

In the U.S. Open, Johnny Miller's 63 in the final

round at Pittsburgh in 1973 stands as the lowest score in the tournament although it is far from being the lowest score returned by a pro. in a major event. Mike Souchak had a 60 as long ago as 1955 when he set the record aggregate of 257 (60,68,64,65) for an American professional tournament in winning the Texas Open. In the course of this achievement he also returned a record score of 27 for nine holes. The only player in the world to equal this performance is Andy North, whose card for nine holes in the British Columbia Open of 1975 read 2,4,4,3,3,3,3,3,2.

Sam Snead had a 59 in the Greenbrier Open at White Sulphur Springs, West Virginia, in 1959, but the lowest score of all for 18 holes in the United States stands at 55. E. F. Staugaard recorded this total with two eagles, 13 birdies and three pars over the 6,419-yard Montebello Park course in California away back in 1935, and Homero Blancas repeated the achievement in 1962 over a shorter 5,002-yard course at Longview, Texas.

Outside of Britain and the United States, the lowest four-round total for a pro. tournament is the 260 (66,62,69,63) returned by Bob Charles in winning the Spalding Masters at Tauranga, New Zealand, in 1969. Gary Player has done a 59 over the 6,185-yard Gavea course at Rio in the Brazilian Open. Jack Nicklaus also had a 59 during an exhibition over a 6,200-yard course at Palm Beach, Florida, in 1973 although, as golf under pressure is not the same game as golf, this performance cannot be ranked in the same class as Player's round in a tournament. For all that, it was a remarkable achievement.

Over the years, there have also been some astonishing feats in the short game. As long ago as 1947, a British golfer named Colin Collen-Smith had an extraordinary round at Betchworth Park, Dorking, where he chipped into the hole on four occasions and single-putted the remaining 14 greens. The U.S. PGA record for the fewest putts in one round stands at 19 and is held jointly by five players: Bill Nary (1952 Texas Open), Bob Rosburg (1959 Pensacola Open), Randy Glover (1965 St. Paul Open), Deane Beman (1968 Costa Mesa Open) and Dave Stockton (1971 Monsanto Open). The record for the fewest putts in one tournament is the 102 (an average of 24.5) recorded by Bert Yancey in the 1966 Portland Open.

Perhaps the most remarkable of these statistics is Staugaard's 55 over a course 6,419 yards in length. Why has nobody been able to match it, or improve upon it, in the intervening 42 years? Why do the record books show that only two players have managed to break 60 in a tournament?

In one sense, golf is a very precise game. The ball has perfect aerodynamic qualities and the clubs are precision instruments, each designed to hit the ball a certain distance if it is struck accurately. On the other hand, the golfer is allowed a reasonable margin of error in terms of direction. Providing a shot is not hooked or sliced, an angle of four or five degrees on either side of his best line will not normally land him in trouble.

Any golfer who can hit the ball straight to a consistent length should therefore be able to play par golf, and any golfer who can hit the ball that little bit harder and be more accurate with his approach shots should be able to play sub-par golf. Yet, if you assemble one hundred of the world's finest golfers for a tournament played in reasonable weather conditions, you cannot expect today that par will be improved upon in more than about 20 of the 400 rounds (or, assuming the normal cut-off, around 300 rounds). Nor is it likely that more than half a dozen, and perhaps even fewer, of the players will return a score below par for the entire tournament.

The conclusion therefore has to be that nobody has yet developed a technique for hitting a golf ball consistently straight and to a consistent length, especially when performing under pressure. All the evidence points to the fact that tournaments are won as a rule by the player who makes the fewest mistakes or the player who is able to add one 'inspired' round to three reasonable rounds. To put this argument another way, after all the years the game has been played golf remains an art rather than what it should be, a science, and, at a conservative estimate, I think it can fairly be said that golf technique lags at least half a century behind the technique of comparable sports.

This situation has arisen because the dominant influence over the evolution of the swing in the last century has been the shape of the golf club. The main effort has been concentrated on making the club easier to control. Unfortunately, with this pragmatic approach you quickly encounter a technique barrier —and it is the failure to pierce this barrier which accounts for golf's comparative lack of progress and why the game remains so difficult to understand and to teach as well as to play.

2: The Technique Barrier

THE suggestion that golf is a purely technical sport and should therefore be a science, not an art, is rarely a popular one at the 19th hole. There, particularly after a disappointing round, members can often be heard to complain: 'We'd all be better off if we just put the ball down and hit it.' This sentiment echoes another oft-repeated maxim to the effect that golf 'is all in the mind.'

Both statements have a fine ring to them and suggest we should all be down to single figures in no time if only we could banish our psychological hang-ups. Unfortunately, both statements happen to be fallacious. The ability to play good golf lies in the body, not in the mind, and the notion of just putting the ball down and hitting it has already been tried and largely, although by no means entirely, abandoned for the very good reason that it does not work consistently well for the vast majority of golfers.

Any discussion of the evolution of the golf swing is complicated by the fact that, at no time in the history of the game, has there been universal agreement about the 'best' method of striking a golf ball. Pictures of the great Harry Vardon, winner of six British Opens (1896, 1898, 1899, 1903, 1911, 1914), show that his body was facing away from the hole at the top of his backswing although, apparently, he ended up facing the hole after the shot. With an 180-degree turn of this kind, I can only imagine that he must have walked into the ball in some way. However, it is certainly a tribute to his innate genius that he was able to play consistent, winning golf over so many years with such an extravagant, and therefore vulnerable, swing.

In contrast, John H. Taylor, one of his two great rivals and winner of the British Open five times (1894, 1895, 1900, 1909, 1913), faced the hole throughout the swing and favoured an open stance with the left toe pointing almost at the flag. Taylor explains in a magazine article in the early years of this century that he adopted this position because it prevented his right elbow from floating up and away from his body on the backswing, a fault which he found to be inevitable if he set himself up with a conventional stance square to the ball.

Today it is equally true that there is no general agreement about the basics of the golf swing. The so-called square-to-square method is usually looked upon as the high point of modern golf technique. Yet Gary Player, who has been known to win the odd dollar here and there, has dismissed it publicly as a lot of nonsense. In the square-to-square method, a weak position for the left hand is advocated. However, Lee Trevino and Billy Casper, two more of the world's most successful tournament players, employ a strong grip instead of a weak one and have the left thumb behind the shot.

Leaving this argument aside for the moment, in order to trace what evolution has taken place in the golf swing over the last century I propose to accept the square-to-square method as the most advanced technique yet developed for golf and compare it with the common characteristics of what can be called the early Scottish swing. This involves going briefly over ground which may be familiar to some readers, but it is important to an understanding of the game and to the latter stages of this book.

If you swing any implement like a golf club, which has an off-centre head, any acceleration produces a rotating force on the hands which the hand muscles try to resist. The first golfers found it natural to swing the club around their bodies, rolling the clubface open on the backswing, bringing it square at impact, and rolling it shut when the ball was on its way. The grip felt comfortable and easy when the club was swung in this manner. It was instinctive to use the arms to generate power, and to whip the hands and hit against a braced body. These early golfers, in fact, did 'just put the ball down and hit it' in the way that came naturally to them and would come naturally today to anyone given a golf club for the first time and asked to swing it. On most golf courses you can see members' children, who have never had a lesson, playing with a swing of this kind and, quite often, playing extremely well.

However, this approach has inherent defects. The arms and hands are relatively weak parts of the body. Consequently, the result can be all too easily a fluff when a golfer is faced with a delicate and difficult shot, particularly if it is a shot which has to be made under pressure in an important medal round, or in a professional tournament when several thousand dollars may hang upon the outcome.

Even more fundamental is the fact that a successful shot depends to a very large degree on co-ordination of hand and eye. This is not too important in the case of children and young adults. With the majority of people, however, the ability to co-ordinate hand and eye begins to diminish in their early twenties. As a result, a golfer using a swing in which the club is taken right around the body and the wrists are allowed to roll freely and rapidly finds it increasingly difficult to have the clubface square to the ball at impact and, consequently, to hit the ball straight. In addition, failure to have the clubface square with this 'natural' swing incurs a double penalty: the pushed shot is also sliced, the pulled shot is also hooked.

The early Scottish swing produced a handful of great golfers whose natural talent enabled them to dominate the game. Obviously, if those of lesser talent were to compete successfully, they had to find a technical means of overcoming the weaknesses inherent in the accepted natural method—the unreliability of the hands and arms as a source of power, and the growing problem, once they were past the first flush of youth, of ensuring that the clubface would be square to the ball at impact.

The result, after several decades of trial and error, has been the square-to-square method and a number of variations of it. It differs in a number of significant ways from the early Scottish swing. The stance is slightly open: the hands are more forward of centre at the address; hip turn has been reduced; the wrists are set at the beginning of the backswing, thus reducing the amount they roll; the club is taken round the body to a lesser degree, with the result that the wrist-rolling that still takes place is much easier to control because of the wide arc of the swing: and—perhaps most important of all—the hips have taken over from the hands and arms as the source of power. The benefits which derive from the modern swing may be summarised as follows:

1. Shots are consistently straighter and even mishits are not so destructive.
2. The quick hook is rare.
3. More pressure can be applied to the ball at

impact, which ensures that it is better flighted (that is, has a more correct relationship between forward spin and backspin), travels further and 'dies' quickly on landing, an important element in accuracy of length.

4. Mistiming causes less damage, the more powerful hips, back and shoulders being capable of dragging the clubhead through the ball in circumstances which would produce a fluff from the weaker hands and arms.

5. This knowledge gives confidence and, as a result, the modern game stands up better under pressure.

The story of the evolution of the golf swing is, of course, by no means as compact and clear as I have presented it here. However, it can safely be said that the basic motivation behind the changes that have taken place has been negative rather than positive. By this I mean that nobody has sat down and said: 'Let's find the best way of using the human body to hit a golf ball.' What they have done is to try to find ways, by experiment rather than analysis, of combating the weaknesses inherent in the early Scottish swing, and the square-to-square method is a distillation of the results of this experimental approach. Consequently, it is open to criticism on a variety of practical, scientific and athletic grounds. Without going into all of these criticisms, I think the following points are sufficient to make it clear that the square-to-square method falls well short of perfection as a means of hitting a golf ball.

● The difficulties involved in hitting a ball with a club which is rotating in two planes simultaneously have been reduced, but not eliminated. The club is still taken around the body; the clubface opens 90 degrees at the top of the backswing; and it has to turn 90 degrees again on the downswing to bring it square to the ball at impact.

If the ball is struck just before the clubface is square, there will be a slight fade; if it struck just after it is square, there will be a slight draw. Even the majority of leading pros. have abandoned any hope of having the clubface square at impact. Instead, they cultivate a deliberate fade or deliberate draw because they feel they can control the ball better if they know which way it will move in the air. This can hardly be regarded as a scientific way of striking the ball.

● The fact that the clubface is rotating means that there still has to be an acceleration of the hands in relation to the body and in relation to each other —that is, a conscious hit with one hand *against* the other—in order to bring the clubface square, or nearly square, at impact. It is often said that this acceleration gives extra power. This is quite false.

Newton's third law of motion states that, to every action, there is an equal and opposite reaction. Therefore, in order to perform any act of propulsion, the part of the body applying the force has to be braced against an adjacent part of the body, and, if a substantial amount of power is required, the process has to continue until the whole body is braced against something solid, usually the earth.

It follows that, if the hands accelerate, they cause an equal and opposite deceleration of the arms. There is therefore no gain in power: it is simply transferred from the arms to the hands. This may not seem very important on the surface. However, it has an important consequence. If the wrists are relaxed, the delicate hands can be used to transmit power and to interpret what happens when the clubhead strikes the ball—that is, to give the feel of the shot, another highly important aspect of accuracy of length. The ability of the hands to transmit feel largely vanishes, however, when the wrists are not relaxed and the hands are used to *apply* force by means of a conscious hit.

The notion of feel, and its importance, is easy to overlook. A convenient analogy may be drawn with what happens inside the mouth of a patient in a dentist's chair. Drilling out a decayed cavity and creating a grip for a filling would be extremely difficult, and frequently impossible, with a hand drill. However, with sophisticated electric drills providing all the power needed, the interpretive hands are able to perform the most sensitive tasks with the utmost ease.

To use the hands for a conscious hit is to ask them to perform a function for which they are ill-equipped and is a cause of many of the disastrous shots seen on golf courses.

● The broad evolutionary trend of the golf swing has been to use progressively stronger muscles as the source of power. First, the hands and arms were used and braced against the shoulders; then the shoulders braced against the back; then the back braced against the hips.

In the modern swing, the hips are used to drive the movement. Leading pros. frequently say in books and magazine articles that they derive their power from the hips *and* legs. It may feel like that to them, but it is not the case. The hips are braced against the legs and the legs are coordinated with the swing because of the understandable reluctance of golfers to disembowel themselves in public.

The logical outcome of this aspect of the evolutionary process would be to use the legs, the most powerful of all the body's muscles, to drive the swing and to brace against the earth. In the modern swing, however, the legs are used only in a negative sense to provide 'the equal and opposite reaction' to the force being generated by the hips.

● The square-to-square method and its variations are not founded on the athletic principles which govern efficient use of the body. No way has been found, for example, of making instinctive use of the strong right side. Instead, the emphasis has been on preventing the strong right side from dominating the swing. The recommended weak position of the left hand on top of the club, for instance, is designed to prevent a hook. For the same defensive reason, the golfer is asked to make a conscious effort to generate the swing by pulling with the left side.

As another example, given the conventional stance, grip and position of the hands at the address, the hips automatically drive the left hand but not the right hand. This problem is overcome by the notion of 'going through in one piece.' In order to go through in one piece, the golfer using the square-to-square method has to contract his muscles and 'hang on' with the right hand. However, the only scientific way to use the muscles to transmit power is to relax them, not contract them.

Another difficulty with the one-piece concept arises when it comes to hitting past the chin. When you have come down in one piece, with the muscles tensed, it is difficult not to come up again in one piece, unless you have the hands much further forward at the address than is the accepted practice today. The outcome is then a hook or, more frequently, a monumental push. There is no prize for guessing the name of the talented young British golfer who has been battling for several seasons now to cure himself of this habit of coming up off the ball.

It requires a great deal of conscious physical effort to keep the clubface travelling behind the ball after impact instead of allowing the wrists to follow their natural inclination to come up and turn over. Exactly how much effort is illustrated by the violent loop at the end of the swing of Arnold Palmer who, despite criticisms of his method, does manage to chase the ball for about a foot after hitting it.

The lack of a truly athletic basis for the modern golf swing is also indicated by the regularity with which modern golfers develop backstrain. Nor does the modern swing cater for the fact that, if the wrists are rolled, the hands have to move in relation to each other on the backswing and downswing. Tournament pros. regularly have to wear protective dressings because of the damage caused by the tendency of the hands to fight each other instead of working together as they do in the two-handed tennis backhand.

● The modern golf swing can never be made a truly natural movement because it is not founded on sound athletic principles. This point also needs some amplification. There are two kinds of natural movement. The first is an instinctive movement, such as the early Scottish golf swing. Then there is the kind of movement which is not in conflict with the body, but has to be made natural by constant repetition. Chopsticks provide a convenient example. The Westerner who encounters chopsticks for the first time finds them extremely difficult to use. However, providing he is prepared to practise, he can eventually become just as accomplished as any Oriental diner.

The square-to-square method does not come into either of these categories. It is not an instinctively natural movement, nor can it be made natural by constant repetition, because the body is in a permanent state of rebellion against what it is being asked to do. Although the square-to-square method has produced far more competent players than any approach tried to date, the modern golfer is always extremely conscious of his swing and produces it mechanically, almost to numbers. It is a swing which lacks flair and can be kept under control only by a combination of constant vigilance and constant practice.

The dominance of Americans in the modern game is not the result of any vast superiority of technique. It arises because there are more golfers in America, which means a greater number of talented young players coming along at any one time, and these young golfers play far more golf—in the sense of practice *and* competitions—than young golfers of other nations. As Syd Scott, the veteran British pro., said on one occasion: 'Today, the young American hoping to make a career in the game has played more four-round medal competitions by the age of 22 than I played in my entire golfing life.'

Only those with the best temperament survive the strains of playing in a succession of highly competitive tournaments which involve constant travelling, living out of suitcases and weekly changes of food and environment. In the circumstances, given the basic flaws in modern golf technique, it is not surprising that the body takes advantage of the occasional touch of fatigue or temporary lapse of concentration to assert itself and execute one of the wild shots which even the greatest players are guilty of from time to time.

Nor is it surprising, in view of the above criticisms, that the square-to-square method is not so compelling that most golfers—or, for that matter, most of the best golfers—feel they must adopt it. Golf therefore remains a highly individualistic game whose essentials are surrounded by uncertainty. It is virtually impossible to make any statement about the swing without starting an argument, and on any golf course—or in any of the top professional tournaments—you can see players still using variations of the early Scottish swing, players using variations of the square-to-square method, players using swings which combine bits of both systems, and players winning tournaments with swings which, if many of the statements made about this complex movement are true, should not strictly speaking work at all.

Tony Lema, the 1964 British Open champion, had the following interesting comments to make about himself and some of his fellow pros. in a magazine article published a couple of years ago:

'If you examine the swings that many of the successful players use, you might well decide that not one of them is any good.

1. Arnold Palmer lunges at the ball and punches it.

2. Jack Nicklaus has the unorthodox habit of letting his right elbow ride far out from his body as he takes the club back.

3. Jacky Culpitt has such a loop at the top of his backswing that it makes him look as though he were waving a flag. I myself loop noticeably at the top.

4. Julius Boros is all hands and wrists like a man dusting furniture.

5. Jerry Barber has his wrists almost completely cocked before he has even started his swing.

6. Doug Sanders braces himself with a wide stance that looks like a sailor leaning into a north-east gale and takes the club back barely far enough to get it off the ground.

If you lined all these players up on the practice tee without knowing who in the world they were and asked them to hit a few shots, your advice would be: "Go back and sell insurance. You haven't got it." '

Top pros. do not merely differ fundamentally from each other in the way they hit the ball. In writing about the game they offer contradictory advice on the correct way of playing it. As I pointed out in *The Golf Swing Of The Future*; 'Tommy Armour says the chip shot is a short jab with a crisp hit with the hands. Gay Brewer, on the other hand, describes the chip shot as a drag movement: he senses that the back of his left hand pushes the club straight back and drags it down through the ball.

'Henry Cotton advocates hitting against a braced left side. Jack Nicklaus and Arnold Palmer both have the left knee bent at the moment of impact with the ball. A highly controversial point is the position of the left wrist at the top of the swing and whether the club-face is open or shut. Leslie King, a leading British teacher, advocates an open clubface at the top of the swing. Most other teachers agree with him. Yet three of Britain's most successful pros., Dave Thomas, Brian Huggett and Neil Coles, all keep the clubface closed.'

The artist who draws a popular instruction strip for one of the world's leading pros. tells me that high-speed camera shots show that the golfer in question does hardly any of the things he advises his readers to do. Another of the world's greatest players urged readers of a golfing magazine recently to stop trying to use the hips and legs as the source of power as they grew older, and to concentrate instead on using the hands and arms. This shows a complete lack of understanding about how the human body works; the hands and arms are not only the weakest part of the body, but the first to lose what strength they have, and to concentrate on using them as you get older can only lead to the loss of so much distance that golf ceases to be worth playing.

In view of the lack of basic athletic and scientific principles in the golf swing today, it is not to be wondered at that the ordinary club golfer finds it difficult to make steady progress at the game. He is faced with conflicting advice, normally stemming from some movement which a pro. has found works for him, although this does not mean that it will work for another golfer, or even another professional golfer.

Hence, the confusion that exists at the level of the club golfer. Some young players get down to scratch in a very short time. Others, often more athletic, practise and practise, yet seem to stick at a handicap of around 15 for their entire playing lives. Many of the young players who were scratch in their 'teens grow steadily worse as the years pass by and have abandoned the game altogether by the age of 50. Furthermore, consistency is a rare quality, and a player off 15 may be nine shots or so better than his handicap one day and nine shots or so worse the next.

Despite my criticisms of the square-to-square method, and the relatively poor standard of most of the golf played in the world today, it would be strange if the golf swing had not given some indication in the course of a century as to where it is trying to go.

The main points in the evolutionary process which has taken place so far are:

- There has been a reduction in the degree to which the club is taken round the body.
- There has been a reduction of hip turn.
- There has been a reduction in rolling of the wrists, both before and after impact.
- There has been a reduction in hitting with the hands.
- The stance has become more open.
- The hands are further forward at the address.
- The trend has been to use more and more powerful muscles to drive the swing.

Projected to their logical conclusion, these developments suggest that, in the ultimate swing, the club would not be taken around the body at all; hip turn, rolling of the wrists and hitting with the hands would be eliminated entirely; the stance would be completely open (as was John H. Taylor's at the turn of the century); the hands would be well forward at the address; and the legs, strongest of all the body's muscles, would be used as the swing's source of power.

It is interesting that a golfer who put all these projections into effect would be well on the way to having a swing which is athletically and scientifically sound. However, golf is prevented from progressing along this path by the technique barrier I mentioned at the end of the last chapter. The breakthrough comes only when you abandon the attempt to work forwards from the shape of the golf club, which has been the dominant influence until now. Instead, you must work backwards from the principles, perfectly understood today, which govern the efficient use of the human body.

3: The Relaxed Way to Power

IF you wish to use the body to propel an object such as a golf ball, the *only* efficient way—and this is now a firmly established principle—is to use the legs as the *sole* source of power. The legs, as I said earlier, are the strongest of all the body's muscles. Even a man who is not very fit can walk all day.

Muscles can transmit more power than they can generate, *providing they are relaxed*. Therefore, in order to use the legs as the source of power, all of the transmission muscles between the legs and hands have to be *relaxed* and *used in reflex*—that is, *without any conscious effort*. As in the case of hitting with the hands, cited in the previous chapter, a conscious movement of any of the transmission muscles sets up an equal and opposite reaction. The reflex chain then breaks down and it is no longer possible to transmit the power directly from the legs at one end of the body to the hands at the other.

In addition, the various parts of the body have to assume *exact positions* before they can be used in reflex. These positions are not natural, in the sense that you would not drop into them automatically. But, unlike the square-to-square swing, they can be made natural by constant repetition because they do not conflict with the way the body works.

This reflex principle has been used to create a perfect technique in field athletics which are, like golf, purely technical sports. The dramatic effect on performances in the course of this century is illustrated by the following table of Olympic results:

SHOT PUTT		JAVELIN	
1900	46ft. 3in.	1908	179ft. 10½in.
1924	49ft. 2¼in.	1924	206ft. 6½in.
1936	53ft. 1¾in.	1936	235ft. 8½in.
1952	57ft. 1½in.	1952	242ft. 0½in.
1968	67ft. 4¾in.	1968	295ft. 7¼in.

DISCUS		POLE VAULT	
1900	118ft. 3in.	1900	10ft. 10in.
1924	151ft. 5in.	1924	12ft. 11½in.
1936	165ft. 7½in.	1936	14ft. 3¼in.
1952	180ft. 6½in.	1952	14ft. 11¼in.
1968	212ft. 6½in.	1968	17ft. 8½in.

The fibreglass pole has, of course, played a significant part in pole vaulting since the last war, but it has only exaggerated the existing trend. Standards in all four events have continued to improve in the last two Olympics. The current records, set in 1976, are: shot putt, 69ft. 11½in.; javelin, 310ft. 4in.; discuss, 224ft.; pole vault, 18ft. 0½in. In the case of the javelin, the improvement during this century is now an astonishing 89 per cent.

These improvements in performance are almost entirely the result of the development of a sophisticated reflex technique. This did not make its appearance overnight, but was the final stage of an evolutionary process which is identical with the evolutionary process we have traced in golf. Initially, the arms and hands provided the power and pushed from a braced body. Then the shoulders were used to generate power, whipping the hands and arms while the legs and hips braced to take the reaction. At the next stage, the power came from the hip muscles and the legs were braced to take the strain.

Each sport then encountered the technique barrier which now faces golf. The barrier arises because of the instinctive way we use our arms. In performing any movement, we have a natural inclination to employ the hingeing action of the elbow. This is a *conscious* movement. The reflex chain breaks down as soon as there is a conscious movement and it is no longer possible to transmit the power directly from the legs to the hands. A way therefore has to be found to eradicate this hingeing action.

In the discus, javelin and shot putt, the problem has been overcome by rotating the right arm (I am speaking, of course, of right-handed athletes) in such a way that it can no longer hinge, but is used instead as a spring. For golf to overcome the same technique barrier, it is necessary to find a right-elbow position in the swing which corresponds to the right-elbow position in these field athletic events.

I think the crucial importance of reflex technique went right over the heads of many, and perhaps even most, of the readers of my first book. It is the *only* way to use the human body at maximum efficiency, and reflex technique is fundamental to the whole method I am about to describe. The main points to be borne in mind when reflex technique is applied to the golf swing are:

- The legs are used as the *sole* source of power.
- The body has to assume a series of *exact* positions.
- The position of the *right elbow* is absolutely critical.
- The transmission muscles between the legs and hands must be *relaxed* in order to apply the power of the legs.
- *No conscious effort* must be made with any of the transmission muscles.

● In particular, there must be *no conscious hit with the hands*, which should be used together, as they are used in the two-handed tennis backhand, and should transmit the power of the legs simply by *dragging the clubhead through the ball*.

Reflex technique is a sophisticated technique. Even learning to grip firmly with the hands while relaxing the other muscles of the body is not a skill you can hope to master in a matter of hours. I am, however, convinced that only the adoption of a soundly-based reflex technique will enable golf to achieve the equivalent of the four-minute mile; eliminate the chaos which surrounds the game today; and provide a pathway to better golf for everyone prepared to take the time and trouble to master the method.

4: The Reflex Swing

THE reflex swing I have developed is not a complicated movement and can be demonstrated in a matter of seconds with a golf club. Describing it in a book is a different matter. It is clear from the amount of correspondence I have been involved in as a result of my previous book that one cannot give too much detail. In this chapter I have therefore tried to anticipate the problems involved in learning a movement from the printed page by giving a very precise account of what happens during the swing. The reader will find some points emphasised over and over again. This is deliberate because I have found that if you mention something once it is inclined to be dismissed as unimportant.

The main points are also repeated in separate captions to the illustrations, partly to re-emphasise them, partly to save the reader from having to keep turning back to look at the text. I am aware that this approach does not make for ease of reading, but I hope there will be a compensatory ease of execution for anyone who wishes to try the swing out.

Even with this detailed and repetitive approach it is easy to leave the reader without an overall impression of the movement or what kind of feeling results from performing it. Before breaking the swing down, it will probably be helpful at this stage to relate it to a simple athletic movement which we have all performed at some time in our lives—skimming a flat stone across the surface of the sea or a lake.

Unlike the normal golfer, the man who wishes to skim a stone on water does not stand sideways to the target and stick his stern out. On the contrary, his left toe points more or less towards the target, the right toe points roughly at right angles to the line of flight, the hips are 45 degrees open, the shoulders are slightly open and the pelvis is thrust forward.

His weight, quite naturally, is placed on the inside of the right foot, which is braced against the earth to absorb the equal and opposite reaction to the throw. His right arm is fairly well forward (across the body) and, although the fingers of the right hand grip the stone firmly, the right wrist is relaxed. From this athletic position, he proceeds to perform a simple athletic movement:

- The left knee moves inwards, towards the line of flight.
- The hips move forward (towards the target) and swivel until they are parallel with the line of flight and can turn no further.
- Simultaneously, the right hand comes back along the line of flight.
- The weight remains on the inside of the right foot.
- The shoulders, which started to turn with the hips, continue to turn after the hips have stopped.
- The right hand continues to go back along the line of flight, *not* around the body.
- The fingers continue to grip the stone firmly but the relaxed right wrist is bent backwards.

In golfing terms, this may be looked upon as the equivalent of the backswing. To throw the stone, the whole movement takes place in reverse. The legs drag the whole body back, the right forearm comes through almost parallel with the ground, and the stone is released. Skimming a stone across water—and, in particular, the shoulder turn involved in skimming a stone across water—is very close to the way the body works in the swing I am about to describe.

My swing is developed from the basic concept of positioning the right elbow so that the power of the legs can be transmitted directly to the hands, as in field athletics events. Figs. 2 and 3 illustrate what is involved. Here we are swinging an outsize club which is too heavy to be swung by the hands alone. The arms are used to hold the club, the left pushing down and the right pulling up to keep the clubhead off the ground.

The right elbow is thrust forward across the body so that the legs can lever the hands. A good angle between the left arm and the club gives control. The left foot is pulled back to maintain balance and there has been a weight-shift to the left to counter the mass of the club. The legs are being used to provide the power and the hands to control the club.

As well as achieving the aim of using the legs, this movement provides several bonuses. Firstly, if the angle is maintained between the left arm and the club, there will be no rolling of the wrists, the curse of the golf swing because it makes it so difficult to hit the ball straight. Even with the square-to-square swing, in which rolling of the wrists has been markedly reduced, top players are always fighting to keep the ball out of trouble, especially when they need that little extra distance. With elimination of wrist-roll, most of the problems involved in hitting the ball straight simply disappear.

Furthermore, all golf shots except the putt are played with backspin, which is essential for length and

Fig. 1. Rolling of the wrists is the curse of the golf swing because it makes it extremely difficult to hit the ball straight. This illustration, based on an action photograph of a leading world player, shows the extent to which the wrists still roll after impact even in the modern golf swing.

control. If you obeyed your instincts in golf, you would try to play the so-called cut-up shot, as in tennis and other ball games when backspin is required. As soon as you roll the wrists, however, you are playing the opposite kind of shot and actually reducing the amount of backspin you can impart to the ball.

Another bonus is feel. It may not be obvious, but a good angle between the club and left arm through the ball is the key to feel. In tennis, for instance, you keep the wrists low for control. Elimination of rolling of the wrists also increases control.

A golf club of normal size can be, but should not be,

swung with the hands alone. It should be swung in exactly the same way as the mammoth club I have been describing. The hands should be passive while the legs provide the power. The weight should move to the left to counter the backswing and the movement through the ball should be a horizontal rotating movement with the wrists low and acting together as a unit. The hands and wrists should not roll—and, providing the right elbow is placed well across the body and a good angle is kept between the left arm and the club, the club can be swung without rolling the wrists.

And so to details.

Posture

Good posture is the foundation of the golf swing. Nearly all the bad shots you see stem initially from bad posture. This is true of top tournament professionals as well as 24-handicappers scuttling the ball along the ground or pursuing an erratic course from rough to sandtrap on a Sunday morning.

It is not possible to strike a golf ball effectively unless the hips are more open than the shoulders at the address. The reason for this is quite simple. Unless the hips are more open than the shoulders they will collapse—that is, turn *with* the shoulders—on the backswing. The body is then like a slingshot when the life has suddenly gone out of the elastic. Muscles are not stretched, the top half of the body is disconnected from the bottom half of the body, and the only way back to the ball is an unathletic yank around with the shoulders.

With the conventional stance the dividing line between a good and bad relationship of the hips and

shoulders is extremely slight. It is therefore not surprising that even top players get it wrong from time to
time and are punished by wild hooks and slices. In
The Golf Swing Of The Future I suggested this problem
could best be overcome by having the shoulders
parallel to the line of flight at the address and turning
the toes of both feet towards the hole, the left foot 30
degrees, the right foot 10 degrees. This created a
good hip-shoulder relationship.

The position of the right foot had the additional
advantage of inhibiting the action of the flexible ball-
joint of the right hip, thus enabling the shoulders to
turn without the hips turning. My ideas on this
matter came in for a good deal of criticism on the
grounds that only a very supple person could turn the
shoulders without turning the hips, and the debate
about the matter focussed my attention on the
question of stance.

Javelin-throwers, discus-throwers and shot-putters
do not stand sideways-on to their direction of flight.
Why should golfers? Within golf itself there was even
some precedence for a much more open stance. John
H. Taylor favoured it long ago; Lee Trevino is 40
degrees open, although this is not commented upon
very frequently because the open position of his feet is
made unobtrusive by the fact that he has his shoulders
open as well; Sam Snead repeatedly made the point
that golf is a very much easier game if a method is
found of getting the left side out of the way; and the
general trend in golf, particularly in the short game,
has been towards a more open stance.

It was a combination of years of brainwashing and
a natural inclination not to be too non-conformist that
prevented me from pursuing this trend to its logical
conclusion. As soon as I decided to take the plunge,
however, a whole lot of things slipped into place. It

became clear that I had been groping towards the stone-skimmer's shoulder turn, which I described at the beginning of this chapter and which is entirely different from the shoulder turn in either the old Scottish swing or the square-to-square swing and is a completely athletic movement which anyone can perform. I also realised that, in some respects, I had been making life unnecessarily complicated, and an open position of the feet made for a swing which, while founded on the principles I put forward in *The Golf Swing Of The Future*, was very much simpler and very much easier to perform.

The Grip

- The grip with the left hand is the old-fashioned two-to-three-knuckle grip (Fig. 4).
- It is a strong, natural fist grip. The line from the base of the thumb to the knuckle of the first finger is at right angles across the shaft of the club.
- The left thumb is down the shaft, a quarter round the grip from the top, and is pulled up slightly.

The position of the left thumb is important because, in sports as diverse as tennis and fishing, you have to have the thumb behind the racket or rod to transmit feel. One of the troubles with the square-to-square method is that you lose feel as soon as you place the left thumb on top of the shaft. For this reason you rarely encounter true flair among golfers using the square-to-square method.

- The grip with the right hand is obtained (see Figs. 5 and 7) by 'screwing on' the middle two fingers of the right hand.

This is the grip which javelin-throwers use. It is also the grip employed by Ben Hogan, probably the finest striker of the ball there has ever been. It allows the right hand to be used in reflex when the club is dragged through the ball, and it counters the rotating effect of the off-centre clubhead.

- The grip with the left hand is firm, but the wrist is relaxed.
- The grip with the middle fingers of the right hand is firm, but the wrist and remainder of the hand are relaxed.
- The left arm pushes down and the middle fingers of right hand pull upwards to maintain a good V-angle between the left arm and the club.
- The pad of the right hand is pulled up from the left thumb.

This is an unconventional grip in the sense that an adjustment has to be made so that the two hands come together in the backswing. I do not think, however, that it is possible to position the right elbow so that the power of the legs can be transmitted directly to the club unless some unconventional grip is used. But the idea of a grip adjustment during the backswing is not as radical as it sounds. In the old-fashioned swing, where the wrists were allowed to roll freely, there was no inclination for either hand to move in relation to the other, but in the modern swing, where rolling of the wrists is restricted, there is a tension between the hands and one or the other has to give, even if only slightly. Therefore, the grip adjustment I recommend merely rationalises the tendency of the hands to fight each other in the modern swing, and for the right hand—accelerating to bring the clubhead square—to hit *against*, not *with*, the left hand.

The grip I have described is a true two-handed grip, corresponding to the two-handed backhand in tennis, and it allows both hands to be used to transmit power directly from the legs to the club providing the wrists are not rolled. The tension created by the action of the two hands—one pushing down, the other pulling up—not only maintains a good V-angle between the left arm and the club, but helps to ensure that the right elbow does not drift away from its proper position across the body at the start of the backswing.

The Address

For any swing, the set-up is all-important, and it is not possible to develop a repeating swing without being able to address the ball in the same way every time. Every golfer should have a definite routine to position himself accurately in relation to the ball and the target, and to enable him to adopt a good posture. It is difficult at any time, and particularly when you are under pressure, to take up a good posture unless you have a very precise routine. Furthermore, when you are under pressure, you will concentrate on your routine and, as a result, take the tension off yourself.

The routine should not be prolonged, but it must be quite definite and it must always be carried out, in practice as well as on the golf course, so that it becomes an integral part of your shot-making. All of the great players have had a clear-cut routine for setting themselves up. There are many possibilities, but the one I have evolved, and recommend, is as follows:

● Stand a few feet behind the ball, grip the club and do a practice swing, or half-swing, to make certain the hands are right.

- Walk up from behind the ball with the head slightly inclined so that you feel you are looking underneath with the right eye. This gives a good set to the body.
- To obtain the line of flight, select a spot about two feet ahead of the ball and in a direct line with the target.
- Place the club behind the ball (Fig. 8) at right angles to the line of flight and with the right elbow well across the body. Feet and shoulders are square and the feet are about 12 inches back from the ball.

In *The Golf Swing Of The Future* I recommended that the clubhead should be placed inside the ball to allow for centrifugal force, which takes the hands away from the body in the golf swing, and for the fact that all the muscles of the body were being relaxed and stretched. With the open position of the feet which I am about to describe, and with the hands off the left leg at the address, it is no longer necessary to make this allowance.

- The left leg is taken back, without moving the shoulders, and turned towards the target (Figs. 9 and 10).
- The left foot points about 10 degrees right of the target.
- The right foot can remain square or be turned about 10 degrees towards the target.
- Lines through the heels to the target would be from five to seven inches apart.
- The weight is distributed equally between the feet, but the right knee is relaxed and pushed slightly towards the hole so that there is a feeling of pressure on the inside of the right foot.
- The shoulders are slightly open, but the hips are very open (roughly 45 degrees).

- The pelvis is well forward.

This is an athletic position of the pelvis and is adopted by modern shot-putters and by modern skiers, who use their legs to generate turns by means of a counter-movement.

- The normal position of the ball is opposite the left instep.

However, as the club does not roll and the clubhead is on line to the target for 18 inches or more, my swing gives a wide range and the ball can be placed as far forward as opposite the left toe (the lowest point of the swing) or as far back as midway between the feet, depending on whether a high or low shot is required.

- The head is in a natural position, with the face turned under so that it points at a spot about two feet ahead of the ball and, if it is turned a little more, it is possible to see the hole, with the left eye vertically above the right eye.
- The trunk has bent to the right slightly to get the head into this position and the head should be as far back (that is, behind the ball) as is comfortable.

In the swing which is about to start, the arms and hands are required to act as a single unit. In order to achieve this tensions have to be set up. Therefore . . .

- The right arm is as far across the body as possible with the inside joint of the right elbow pointing away from the body (that is, in the 'spring' position).
- The left arm is inside the vertical, looking at it from the target (Fig. 10).
- The elbows are pressed together.
- The left arm continues to push down and the

middle two fingers of the right hand pull up to maintain a good V-angle between left arm and club, and the feeling is that the two middle fingers of the right hand pull against the left thumb.

In a normal swing, the club is at right angles to the line of the hips. My position is very different. I feel as if I am in the position shown in Fig. 3, but with the hands lower and what could be described as a side-saddle grip.

The Press

If the posture is correct, practically all faults in the golf swing stem from the method of starting it. It is essential to understand what a swing is. A great deal has been written about swinging the club, as distinct from lifting it up and hitting with it, and it has been said that it is like swinging a weight on the end of a piece of string. This is not the case.

With a weight on the end of a piece of string, you have to move the centre of rotation to increase the centripetal force. A mental picture of a man whirling a lasso will clarify what I mean. In the golf swing we are concerned with the opposite of centripetal force— centrifugal force, or force tending to go away from you.

The essential part of the swing is the building up of the centrifugal force of the club and body by using your muscles to accelerate the speed of rotation about a *fixed* point. In the golf swing, the fixed point of rotation is the neck, which should stay still throughout the swing. This is not a matter of 'freezing' the neck. It is a question of starting the swing in such a way that the neck will automatically remain in the same relationship to the ball.

It is not possible to do this repeatedly if you start the swing by a conscious effort from a stationary position. Such a conscious effort with one part of the body tends to move the other parts of the body. It involves a contraction of muscles which exert a force on whatever part of the body they are pulling against. In the golf swing they are pulling against the neck and tending to move it.

The swing must therefore always be started with a press of some kind. A press is the tensing of muscles in a stationary position so that the swing starts, without any tendency to contract the muscles, as soon as the muscles are relaxed. The type of forward press dictates which part of the body is used to strike the ball. If you press with the hands, you will hit with the hands; if you press with the right hip, you will hit with the hips; if you press with the legs, you will use the legs as the source of power providing the rest of the body is in the correct position.

I press with the right leg. Having set myself up, I . . .

- Look at the target by turning my head so that my left eye is almost vertically above the right eye.
- Then, before starting the swing, I do a push with the right leg.

This is quite a definite and deliberate movement, making the legs feel alive, and it is the same movement you would perform instinctively before throwing a stone.

I have previously mentioned looking underneath with the right eye when you first approach the ball. Before the press I have now recommended looking at the target by turning the head so that the left eye is almost vertically above the right eye. This matter of looking underneath is important and needs elaboration.

It is almost impossible to feel slight mistakes in the set-up of the body which could produce an indifferent shot if the feeling of looking under at the target is ignored. If, for example, the head and shoulders are turned too much towards the target at the address, the legs will pull the body round and the head will come up. Turning the head to look at the target, with the right eye under the left eye, will correct this and other errors if they have crept in unnoticed.

Turning the head in this way is a deliberate check for correct posture. In fact, the position of the head at the address—facing a point about two feet ahead of the ball—should be such that the ball, the target and, most important, the line from the ball to the target, can all be seen simply by turning the eyes.

The reason for this is that, when you are striking a ball which you know will be propelled in a certain direction, it is difficult to stop your inclination to anticipate the movement. With the head in the recommended position and able to follow the ball moving only the eyes, there should be no temptation to look up, and interfere with the mechanics of the swing, as the club is swung through the ball.

The Takeaway

Assuming the set-up is reasonably reliable, a repeating swing depends on the press and takeaway being exactly the same each time. The first movement is shown in Figs. 11 and 12. In the normal swing, there is a weight-shift to the right and then a move into the ball. My movement is the opposite. I push the club away from me so that I can pull it through the ball, and I counter this movement by shifting my weight to the left. Again, this is the same movement you would use in throwing a stone. Therefore, after the press . . .

- The swing is started by an instinctive movement of the legs, which push the club straight back from the ball.
- The hips move towards the target and swivel 45 degrees until they are parallel to the line of flight.
- If the pelvis is forward and the club is not taken around the body, the hips will automatically cease to turn once they have reached this position.

As the technique I am describing is basically about the position of the right elbow—well across the body —in which it can transmit the power from the legs, maintaining this position has to be the main aim throughout the swing. The basic problem is to avoid taking the club around the body and allowing the right elbow to 'escape' in the process.

Until such time as the movements have been made natural (or muscle-memorised) by constant repetition, it is important to concentrate on what the hands and arms are doing in the takeaway. Used correctly, they prevent the right elbow from straying and, if anything, force it more across the body than it was at the address.

- The press of the right leg tenses the right hand and, as the legs start the swing, the left hand pushes the club under the right hand, which bends fully back on the first movement. This is helped by the two middle fingers of the right hand pulling against the left thumb. The hands are well out from the body as they pass the right knee.
- The first movement of the right arm is all-important. Fig. 13 shows how the right arm turns

clockwise at the start of the takeaway, but the movement is hidden in Figs. 11 and 12.

In fact, this means that the left hand pushes the club straight back with the clubface remaining at right angles to the line of flight. This is normally referred to as 'hooding the club', but it is actually a truly square method which eliminates the complications that arise when you are trying, as in the conventional golf swing, to strike a ball with an implement which is rotating in two planes—around the body and around the arms—simultaneously.

The position of the wrists is also important in transmitting the power to the club.

- The back of the left hand is rounded, or bowed, from the start, not cupped, with the back of the left hand facing away from the body.
- This gives a set to the left hand and bends the right hand backwards from the wrist into a flexed position.
- The action of the two hands together exerts pressure on the right elbow, forcing it more towards the centre of the body.

The elements of this movement can be simulated by standing with the right arm well across the body and the palms together, horizontal to the ground. If the right hand is pushed backwards from the wrist by the left hand, the right elbow is immediately forced more across the body.

The bowed position of the left hand at the start of the swing corresponds to the modern one-handed tennis backhand position, in which the wrist is not rolled, and it must be retained throughout the swing. Any inclination for the left hand to be cupped rather than rounded is fatal. This set of the left hand, and the resulting set of the right hand, is also, incidentally, essential to the square-to-square method.

To summarise, the swing begins with a press (by the right leg) followed by the takeaway, in which the legs swing the trunk to the right and the undercarriage slides to the left to balance it.

The feeling is that the top part of the body is rotating around the right hip-joint.

The Backswing

At the halfway stage of the swing, when the hips have moved forward and are parallel with the line of flight, and the hands have just passed the right hip, the main points you should have concentrated on to ensure that the movement has been executed correctly are:

- That the right elbow is still well across the body.
- That the left wrist is bowed.
- That the back of the hand is still visible out of the corner of the eye although the head has not moved.

It is important to remember that, up to this stage of the swing, the hands move roughly parallel with a line across the toes of the two feet.

- As the left hand pushes the club straight back, the action of keeping the clubface square to the line of flight causes the left hand to turn anti-clockwise, with the left thumb moving up and over.
- The left thumb then 'locks' quite naturally in the V at the base of the right hand, creating a firm grip which is maintained throughout the swing.
- The shoulders complete a 90-degree turn from

square after the hips have stopped and the movement is the same as the stone-skimmer's turn, a
simple athletic movement.

● The hands are still being pushed back along
the line of flight and the feeling is that you are about
to take part in a tug-o'-war with someone who is
holding the clubhead.

To summarise again . . .

By the time the backswing is half-completed, the
position of the right elbow is secure and the hands
have come together. The arms, with the right elbow
well across the body and well into the body, form a
rigid structure, coupling the hands and clubs to the
body.

The main feeling of the backswing is that I have
swung the top part of the body to the right and countered it with a slide of the hips to the left (Fig. 14).
The clubhead has been swung straight back from the
ball, the face of the club remaining square to the line
to the target. The hands feel as if they are out in
front of the body. The left hand is quite tight with
the back of the left hand rounded, and the left
thumb feels as if it is on top of the club.

The Top Of The Swing

At the top of the swing (Fig. 15), I feel that I have
swung the trunk and arms as far to the right as I can,
using the legs as a counterbalance. At the top of the
swing . . .

● At the top of the swing the two middle
fingers of the right hand are pulling against the
left thumb, giving the feeling of turning the club
anti-clockwise.

● Although the muscles are relaxed, the arms

feel 'welded' into one piece with the elbows close together.

- The head has not moved. The right eye is still slightly underneath the left eye. Both the ball and the spot two feet or so in front of it are still visible.

I have achieved a position where I feel that the hands and arms are stretched and any movement of the legs will drag the clubhead back to the ball. The right arm position shown in Fig. 16 has made this possible.

The Downswing

The term 'downswing' is a misnomer. It is actually a downward drag which is a combination of two movements—a horizontal rotating movement, led by the legs, which drags down the hands—and it is the backswing in reverse.

- The feeling is that the right hip is pulling the hands straight down through the ball with the clubhead trailing.
- To counter the clockwise rotating effect of the off-centre clubhead, the hands must keep up an anti-clockwise pressure, giving the feeling of shutting the clubface.
- The grip is still firm.
- As the hands approach the right hip, the hips start to swivel back to their address position, 45 degrees open.

From the top of the swing, the downward drag (Fig. 17) is a one-piece movement. The feeling is that the hands and the right shoulder are together and they come down into the ball as one. I have the impression that I am making contact with the ball with my right shoulder behind the right forearm.

It is not possible to get this feeling unless the head is behind the right hip—that is, the hip has moved to the left on the backswing. This is the reason why the pelvis has to be forward at the address. If the stern is sticking out, you cannot turn *over* the right hip on the backswing, which is, in effect, what I have done.

The feeling of making contact with the ball with the right shoulder ensures that my head stays back and that the hands are passive. It also ensures that I go right under—that is, with the right eye coming up under the left eye.

Through The Ball

At impact with the ball, there is still no conscious effort to use the body or, worst of all, to hit with the hands.

- The hands do not roll over, but remain in the same relationship to each other—as in the two-handed tennis backhand—while the legs *drag* them together through the ball.
- The flexed hands provide the feel of the shot.
- The shoulders are nearly vertical at impact.
- The right forearm comes through almost horizontal at impact.
- The head turns in a vertical plane (the right eye immediately under the left), which prevents any tendency to pull round with the shoulders and enables you to watch the clubhead go through the ball.
- The hands continue their backswing path in

reverse (roughly parallel to a line across the toes) without rolling over. However, the *feeling* is that the hands go towards the hole.

● The clubhead *does* continue to travel towards the hole and does not catch up with the hands until after the arms have been extended as far forward as possible.

The feeling through the ball is that the hands have been dragged down over the ball, well away from the body, with the club trailing. That is, the hands seem to pass the chin and over the ball well before impact.

I have avoided using the word 'hit' and, instead, employed the word 'impact' and the expression 'dragging the club through the ball.' There is a fundamental difference, which I analysed in Chapter II with the analogy of the dentist's drill, but which is so important that it is worth repeating.

With a hit, I think of bracing the body and tightening the wrists so that the hands or arms can deliver a blow. However, the hands are too feeble to *apply* force directly and the scientific approach is to drag the club through the ball. This means you are bracing against the ground and the wrists are relaxed so that they can be used in reflex (with no conscious effort) to *transmit* the power of the legs to the ball and generate maximum pressure. It is essential to have the feeling that impact with the ball is a dragging movement if you are to use the legs effectively.

The modern golfer using the square-to-square method avoids hitting with the right side and drags the club through the ball to a much greater degree than earlier golfers. Consequently, accuracy of length is much greater than it used to be.

I go into the reasons for this in greater detail in the subsequent section on clubhead speed v. pressure when contact is made with the ball. Meantime, it is worth making the point that probably the greatest striker of the ball there has ever been, Ben Hogan, dragged the clubhead through the ball for all his shots. Today, Lee Trevino, who is also very straight and has tremendous control, is the player with the greatest mastery over this technique. In his recent book, *Groove Your Golf Swing My Way*, he explains how he came to realise that Hogan was playing a different game from everybody else and decided to model himself upon him:

'There was a time when I played golf the way all the books and most of the teachers since Harry Vardon have said you're supposed to play. I had a "square" stance. I swung the club around my body, keeping my right elbow in tight, of course. And I tried to uncock my wrists at impact, not too early, not too late.

'Well, I soon found out that they just didn't build courses big enough—at least, not *wide* enough—for my game. I covered more Texas real estate than Davy Crockett, Sam Houston and L.B.J. put together. Every round was like a cattle drive.

'Then one day I had a chance to watch Ben Hogan practice . . . I just sat and watched him manoeuvre the ball—high shots, low shots, draw shots, fades. He hit shots of every shape you could imagine, and they all finished so close together out there that his caddie could have been a blind man on crutches.

'The thing I really watched as Hogan hit these shots was how he used his hips and legs. I remember getting a clear impression that he controlled his shots with his lower body . . .'

Trevino began hitting as many as a thousand golf balls a day in his successful attempt to develop a similar technique: 'This routine led to divorce, but it sure taught me how to control a golf ball . . . I developed a swing that isn't the prettiest thing you'll ever see, and it certainly isn't orthodox, but I think it's the most *functional* golf swing around . . .'

From the point of view of the reflex technique I have described, the methods employed by Ben Hogan and Lee Trevino cannot be considered 100 per cent pure. The wrists pronate slightly so, even if only to a minor extent, there has to be a hit with the hands, but fundamentally both of them drag the club through the ball and this is the foundation of their success.

When I think of dragging the clubhead through the ball, it makes me pause at the top of the swing as I am bracing against the inertia of the club. Then, when I drag the clubhead through the ball with the legs, I have the whole weight of the body behind it because I am still pulling at impact (Figs. 18 and 19).

At impact, it feels as if the clubhead and hands go through the ball as a unit. The feeling of having a good angle between the arms and club is a 'must'. The impact impression is that the ball has been picked up and catapulted at the target, and the contact is very solid.

It is at impact that the importance of the very open stance becomes evident. Unless the left leg is drawn well back, it is not possible for the legs to drag the right shoulder down and through the ball. The open feet and hips also make it very much easier to generate and control the speed of the clubhead.

It is the centripetal (coming toward you) force of the hands as they pull across a line roughly parallel with the toes which generates the centrifugal (going away from you) force of the clubhead and makes it pick up speed. With an open stance and the centre of gravity well inside the right foot, there is plenty of room to pull without dislocating the swing. In contrast, the centrifugal force of the clubhead is very difficult to control in the conventional swing and there is a pronounced tendency for the player to be pulled up off the ball, particularly when he is trying for that little bit of extra length.

The Follow-Through And Finish

At impact, the body is almost facing the target and the arms and club then feel as if they are flung up after the ball although, as I have said, this is not actually the case with the hands. The hands still lead at the end of the swing and the head has stayed back. At the finish (Fig. 21), the hands are high and you should be looking at the target with the right eye lower than the left eye.

●   ●   ●

Much of this chapter is meant to be read standing up, with a golf club in your hand, rather than relaxed in an armchair. It has taken a lot of words to describe the reflex swing in detail, but the following illustrations, with their more concise captions, should make it clear that the movement is not as complicated as it may have sounded up to now.

Figs. 2 and 3.   Visualise the Swing
You would swing a golf club in quite a different way if it was too heavy to be swung by the hands alone. Here:

● The arms are used to hold the club, the left pushing down and the right pulling to keep the clubhead off the ground.
● The right elbow is thrust forward across the body so that the legs can lever the hands.
● A good angle between the left arm and the club gives control.
● The left foot is pulled back to maintain balance and there has been a weight shift to the left to counter the mass of the club.
● The legs are being used to provide the power and the hands to control the club.

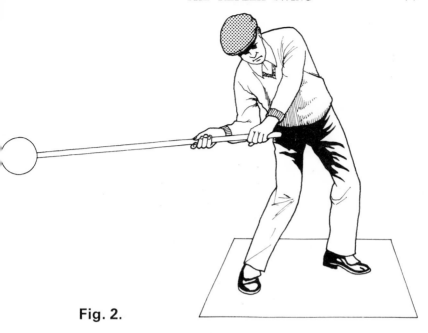

Fig. 2.

Fig. 3.

All of these points are important elements of the reflex swing with an ordinary club.

Figs. 4, 5, 6 and 7.   The Grip

● The grip with the left hand is the old-fashioned three-knuckle grip. It is really a fist grip with the thumb down the shaft, but pulled up slightly, and a quarter round the shaft from the top (Fig. 4).

● The middle two fingers of the right hand are screwed on to the club (Figs. 5 and 7).

● The pad of the right hand is pulled up from the left and the hands come together during the backswing.

This grip enables me to get the right elbow further across the body at the address.

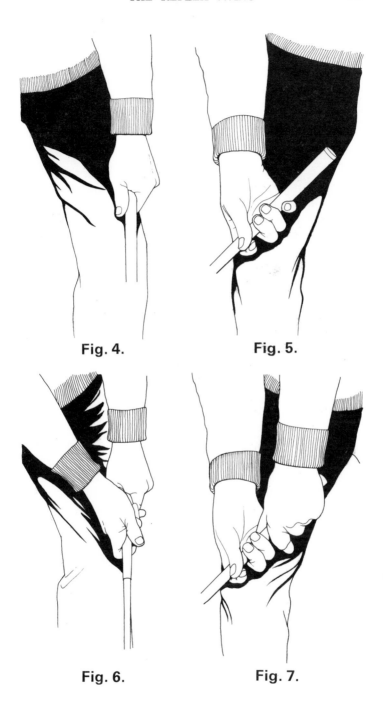

Fig. 4.

Fig. 5.

Fig. 6.

Fig. 7.

Figs. 8, 9 and 10. The Address

It is not possible to have a repeating swing unless you address the ball in the same way every time. You must therefore have a definite routine.

- Stand behind the ball and check the grip with a swing, or half-swing, of the club.
- Walk up behind the ball with the head slightly inclined so that you feel you are looking underneath with the right eye.
- To establish the line of flight, select a spot about two feet ahead of the ball and in line with the target.
- Place the club behind the ball at right angles to the line of flight (Fig. 8). The right elbow is well across the body and the feet are about 12 inches back from the ball.
- The left leg is taken back and turned towards the target (Fig. 9).
- The left foot points about 10 degrees right of target, the right foot from square to 10 degrees left of square to the line of target.
- Lines through the heels to the target would be five to seven inches apart.
- The shoulders are slightly open, but the hips are about 45 degrees open.
- The pelvis is well forward.
- The head faces the spot about two feet ahead of the ball and the trunk has bent slightly to the right to get the head in this position. The head should be as far back as is comfortable.
- The ball is opposite the instep of the left foot.
- The weight is evenly distributed between the feet, but the right knee is pushed very slightly inwards towards the hole so that there is a feeling of pressure on the inside of the right foot.
- The elbows are pressed together.
- The left arm pushes down and the middle fingers of the right hand pull up, to maintain a good V-angle between the left arm and the club.
- The left arm is inside the vertical, looked at from the target (Fig. 10).

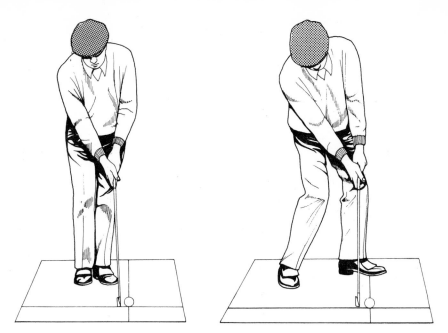

Fig. 8.   Fig. 9.

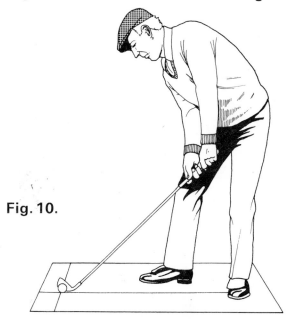

Fig. 10.

The arms and hands are required to act as a single unit throughout the swing and the tensions between them, which have been set up at the address, must therefore be maintained throughout the swing.

Figs. 11, 12 and 13.   The Takeaway
A repeating swing also depends on the takeaway
being the same each time.

  ● Look at the target with the right eye
almost vertically below the left eye.
  ● Press with the right leg to make the legs
feel alive. This press tenses the right hand and,
as the legs start to swing, the left hand pushes
the club under the right hand, which bends
fully back on the first movement. The movement is helped by the two middle fingers of
the right hand pulling against the left thumb
and bowing the wrist.
  ● The hands are well away from the body
as they pass the right knee.
  ● The right arm turns clockwise at the start
of the takeaway (Fig. 13). This is the only
movement which will keep the right elbow in
position well across the body.

The feeling of the takeaway is that the top part
of the body is rotating around the right hip-joint.

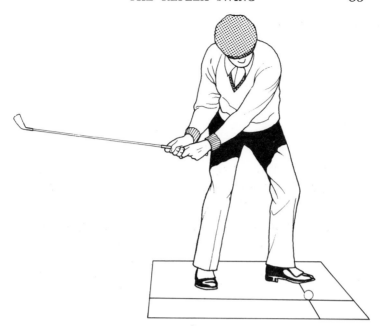

Fig. 11.

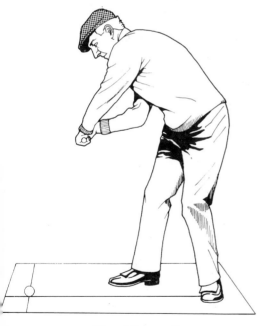

Fig. 12.

Fig. 13.

Fig. 14. The Backswing

The main feeling on the backswing is that I have swung the top part of the body to the right and countered it with a slide of the hips to the left.

- The clubhead is swung straight back from the ball with the clubface square to the line to the target.
- The hands have come together by the time the backswing is half-completed and feel out in front of the body.
- The left hand is quite tight, with the back of the hand bowed, and the left thumb feels as if it is on top of the club.
- The two middle fingers of the right hand pulling against the left thumb give the feeling of turning the club anti-clockwise.

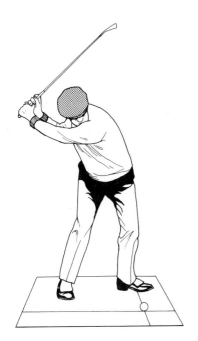 

Figs. 15 and 16.   The Top of the Swing

At the top of the swing (Fig. 15) I feel I have swung the trunk and arms as far to the right as I can, using the legs as a counterbalance. It is like a tug-o'-war. The right hand is behind the club.

Fig. 16 shows the right elbow position which will transmit the leg power to the hands. The inertia of the club has forced the right hand back and thrust the right elbow further across the body. In this position, any pressure from the legs is transmitted to the hands.

● Although the muscles are relaxed, the arms feel 'welded' into one piece with the elbows close together.

● The head has not moved. The right eye is still slightly underneath the left eye. Both the ball and the spot two feet or so in front of it are still visible.

Fig. 17.   The Downswing

The downswing, or downward drag as I prefer to call it, is the backswing in reverse. The right hip pulls the hands straight down through the ball with the club trailing.

- The right elbow is still in position across the body.
- The pressure is still on the inside of the right foot.
- The hands keep up an anti-clockwise pressure to keep the face of the club square.

The downward drag is a one-piece movement. The feeling is that the hands and the right shoulder are together and they come down into the ball as one. I have the impression that I am hitting the ball with my right shoulder behind the right forearm.

It is not possible to get this feeling unless the head is behind the right hip: that is, the hip has moved to the left on the backswing. This is why the pelvis has to be forward at the address. Otherwise you cannot turn over the right hip on the backswing, which, in effect, is what I have done.

The feeling of hitting the ball with the right shoulder makes sure that the head stays back and the hands are passive. It also ensures that you go right under, with the right eye coming up under the left eye and the right shoulder coming up under the right eye.

Fig. 17.

Figs. 18 and 19. Through the Ball

The legs drag the right shoulder down and through the ball. There is no attempt to make a conscious hit. The feeling of having a good angle between the arms and the club is essential.

- The left wrist is still bowed.
- The right hand is still flexed.
- The grip is firm.
- The hands do not roll over, but remain in the same relationship to each other, as in the two-handed tennis backhand.
- The shoulders are nearly vertical at impact.
- The right forearm comes through almost horizontal at impact.
- The hands feel as if they go towards the hole although, in fact, they travel across the body on a path roughly parallel with a line across the toes.
- The clubhead *does* continue to travel towards the hole.

The feeling through the ball is that the hands have been dragged down over the ball, well away from the body, with the hands trailing. That is, the hands seem to pass the chin and over the ball well before impact.

Fig. 18.

Fig. 19.

Figs. 20 and 21. The Follow-through and Finish

After impact, the arms and club as a unit feel as if they are flung up after the ball although, as I have said, the hands actually travel across the body. The hands still lead until the end of the swing. The head has stayed back. At the finish, the hands are high and you should be looking at the target with the right eye lower than the left.

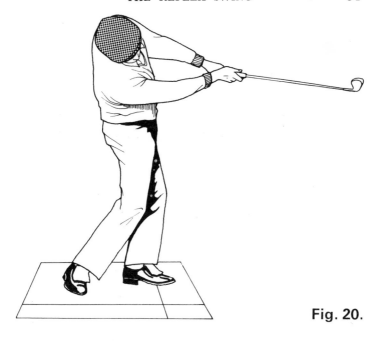

Fig. 20.

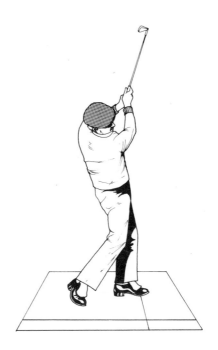

Fig. 21.

This reflex golf swing corresponds to the scientific techniques which have led to such dramatic improvements in the performances of field athletes, and it is, I believe, the ultimate form which the golf swing will take. The *exact* positions you have to adopt in executing the swing are not natural positions in the sense that you would drop into them automatically. However, nor are they in conflict with the way the body works. They can therefore be made natural by constant repetition, just as we make writing, using a knife and fork, and other daily movements natural by constant repetition.

The main advantages of such a reflex swing can be easily summarised. It enables the legs, strongest of all the body's muscles, to power the swing; it eliminates rotation of the clubhead; and it eliminates all need to hit with the highly suspect hands.

Anyone wishing to try out the reflex swing should begin with chips for the obvious reason that a wedge or 8-iron is very much easier to control than a driver. I have dealt with the matter of chip-shots in the section on the approach to the game. First of all, however, I feel it is important to consider whether clubhead speed or pressure is the more desirable quality when you make contact with the ball.

5: Clubface Speed v. Pressure

CONTACT between the golf club and the golf ball has inspired millions of words and almost every golf book talks about getting maximum clubhead speed as the secret of length.

It is true that, by whipping the hands and getting maximum speed of the clubhead, a golf ball can be hit a long way. For the young it is an instinctive way to hit a ball. With co-ordination of hand and eye, they can play tunes with a golf club, and the split-second timing required with a rolling clubface presents few difficulties. However, when co-ordination of hand and eye begins to fade in the early twenties, a golfer finds he has to rebuild his game on a more technical method if he is ever to play again to his former standard. This process explains why so many talented teenagers do not fulfil their early promise and why so many of the great players, having persevered in their quest for a technical method and finally mastered it, do not reach their peak before the late thirties or even their forties.

To my mind, there are two extremes to the method of making contact—the high-speed swing and the high-pressure swing—and the high-pressure swing is the superior. Only a young player can swing a golf club fast enough to match the distance obtained with a high-pressure swing. Furthermore, the high-pressure swing provides not only length, but accuracy of length. The reasons for this can be seen when the two approaches are analysed.

With the high-speed swing, the golfer winds up on the backswing and unwinds on the downswing so that the clubhead is travelling as fast as he can make it travel. At this speed, all the power is in the inertia of the clubhead, which is acting as a projectile. When it collides with the ball, its speed is reduced from, say, 100 m.p.h. to 80 m.p.h.

With the high-pressure swing, the golfer takes the club to the top of the swing and winds *up* on the downswing so that his muscles are stretched at impact and he exerts maximum pressure. The clubhead may be travelling at only, say, 85 m.p.h., but its speed will not drop below 80 m.p.h. on contact with the ball.

The ball is probably on the clubface for three quarters of an inch with the high-speed swing. With the high-pressure swing, the distance increases to more than an inch. Despite the slower swing, length is not reduced because you are applying force through a distance instead of just causing a collision.

There is also a bonus with the high-pressure swing. The shaft of the club bends slightly in the downswing and bends a little more on contact with the ball. The ball, in its turn, is squashed. Therefore, the longer you can keep the clubhead and ball together, the more bonus power you obtain as the shaft of the club straightens and the ball returns to its normal shape.

The truth of this argument is more easily seen in tennis where you get nowhere if you just flap at the ball. To obtain a solid, powerful stroke you have to apply pressure to the ball by accelerating the racket, with a firm grip, *after* impact. The ball and racket strings are then in contact for three inches or more.

In golf, the fact that the club is much heavier and does not have flexible strings tends to mask the validity of applying this principle to the game. Nevertheless, pressure—the application of force through a distance—should be used in exactly the same way in golf.

The backswing and downswing should be relatively slow with the club accelerating steadily as it comes into the ball. A slow swing of this kind is easier to control; the fact that the clubhead and ball are in contact over a greater distance gives the body more time to transmit the feel of the shot to the brain; and applying pressure to the ball ensures that it is correctly flighted.

Correct flighting means that you impart the correct amount of backspin to keep the ball in the air while the momentum of the shot is carrying it forwards. The importance of pressure in correct flighting is revealed at once when you watch most women players. They rarely flight the ball well because their hands and wrists are not strong enough to keep up the pressure at impact. As a result, much of their distance is achieved by the ball rolling along the ground where it is at the mercy of awkward bounces.

In contrast, if the ball is well flighted with plenty of backspin, it 'dies' quickly on landing. It is clear that, providing you know the ball will 'die' on landing, you have much more exact control over accuracy of length, and you can use the different clubs in the way they are intended to be used—as precision instruments.

The way golf is played today, there are just as many speed-pressure ratios among players as there are varying golf swings. Broadly-speaking, however, the swing where the clubface opens at the top of the swing and the left wrist is cupped is usually the high-speed swing, and the more modern swing with the flat left wrist tends towards the pressure end of the scale.

The reflex swing I have outlined goes right to the

end of that scale with the power of the legs being used
to exert maximum pressure at impact. In addition, it
is not a defensive swing in that I can hit with the right
side and, as the club does not roll over, employ maximum effort without fear of lapses in direction. It is
also a technique which produces flair and touch with
chips, pitches and half-shots, as well as providing an
excellent putting method.

6: The Approach to the Game

TO play good golf it is important to have a clear and positive approach to each department of the game.

The Drive

Anyone whose reputation rests simply on long hitting is seldom a good competitor. The object with the tee shot should be reasonable and consistent length, accuracy of direction and confidence that you have the power and ability to hit the ball that bit harder when necessary.

Most modern courses, and the good ones in particular, are designed for a positioned tee shot on the long holes, both from the point of view of making the second shot easier and from the fact that fairways tend to narrow around 220 or 230 yards and threaten trouble to the shot that is slightly off line and does not 'die' quickly.

Even on the hardest and driest fairway, the well-flighted shot will not run unduly far after landing. When Ben Hogan was playing in a tournament, you would find his tee shots at the long holes ending up in much the same spot in each of the four rounds. This is what everyone should aim at. It has the additional advantage that you can establish how short or how long the course is playing by using your tee shot as a measure.

The Fairway Wood

This, too, should be a precision shot. It is important to be straight, but it is even more important to hit an accurate length. If your length tends to vary widely, you are uncertain which club to take. Correct flighting to obtain distance through the air is vital.

For example, take a situation in which you are faced with a distant bunker, followed by 50 yards of fairway to the green. If your wood shots normally run 45 yards after landing, you must pitch the ball just over the bunker in order to reach the green. On the other hand, if you know the ball will 'die' within 10 yards of landing, you have 40 yards of fairway to play with. On most good courses there is no problem if you hit an accurate length that is all carry.

The Irons

With the irons you should be aiming to get close enough to the pin to finish with a single putt. It is obvious that you have to be reasonably straight, but the important aspect of iron play is again accuracy of length. The player who has to play short of an open green because he knows the ball will run is always at the mercy of a bad bounce, and he can never go for the pin with any confidence.

The irons are designed to give a variation of distance of from 10 to 15 yards, depending on the strength of the player. To achieve this degree of accuracy, it is essential to hit the ball correctly. The inclination, particularly with the shorter irons, is to hit the ball flat on the face of the club, which means that you get several yards more distance with the shot than either you or the clubmaker envisaged.

When the club is placed on the ground, you should imagine a plane at right angles to the ground from the front edge of the club. It is this plane (Fig. 22) which you should feel strike the ball if you are going to flight it properly and achieve the correct distance.

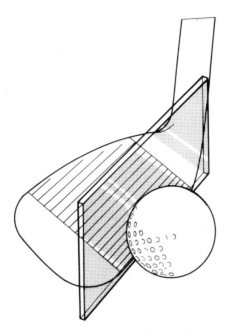

Fig. 22.

It is difficult to do this consistently with the early golf swing, in which there was pronounced rolling of the wrists and timing was consequently critical, and even today, when rolling of the wrists has been reduced and takes place over a much wider arc, it is still by no means easy.

The aim with the irons should be to know precisely which club you need, and to be reasonably certain that, if you pitch the ball on the green, it will stay there.

The Chip

If you feel you can get down in two from around the green providing you concentrate, you can win almost any match. Chipping straight is not all that difficult. It is accuracy of length that is important because, with the chip, you should be going for the hole, not merely for the green.

You may say that these standards are impossible for the part-time golfer. I do not agree. Accuracy of length, the most important aspect of all golf shots, is simply a matter of good technique and practice. There is no short cut to good golf. Developing a technique is a protracted task. Yet it is only by adopting and mastering a sound technique that steady progress can be made at the game.

Anyone trying out the technique I have put forward should begin by applying it to chips. My approach is as follows:

The Address

The address (Figs. 23 and 24) is the same as for the full shot. My head faces about two feet in front of the ball and I have the feeling of looking underneath with the right eye. The weight is on my heels and I have a good firm grip of the club. The left arm pushes down and the right arm pulls against it.

In Fig. 23, the left arm is shown slightly more inside the vertical (looked at from the target), because it can make the delicate shot easier if the hands are pulled in towards the left knee and you stand a little closer to the ball.

216090

The Backswing

The backswing (Figs. 25 and 26) is the same as for the long shot and the swing is a miniature of the full swing. That is why I suggest the feel of the fundamentals of my swing can be most easily obtained by at first doing simple chips to numbers.

(1)   From the address position to Figs. 25 and 26, I press with the right leg and as in the full swing, the left hand pushes the club under the right hand, straight back from the ball.

(2)   The hands have come right out from the body and the right hand is behind the club with the right elbow almost into the stomach.

(3) The hips have moved to the left and turned, and are braced to pull the clubhead through the ball by the simple movement of swinging round. It can be seen that a good angle between the left arm and the club is essential.

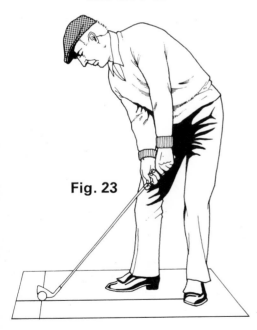

Fig. 23

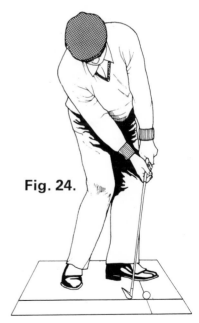

Fig. 24.

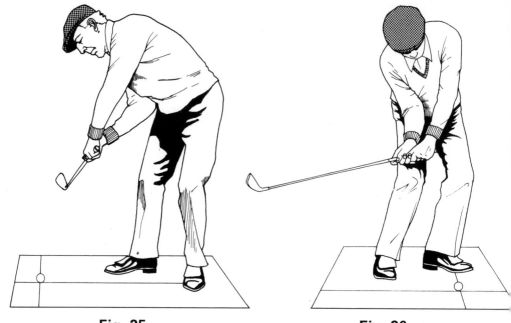

Fig. 25.

Fig. 26.

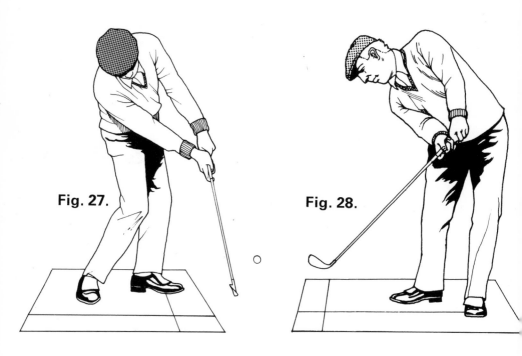

Fig. 27.

Fig. 28.

Through The Ball

(4)   The legs have dragged the club through the ball (Figs. 27 and 28).

(5)   The body, arms and club are all in one piece.

(6)   The feeling has been that the hands and club are an extension of the right shoulder.

(7)   The right shoulder has gone under the right eye which has gone under the left eye.

This is a simple movement, but to be able to hang on firmly with the hands, while at the same time having enough relaxation of the arms and wrists to swing the club back and drag it through the ball, requires many hours of practice. However, it can be made into a relaxed and natural movement, which gives much greater control than any other technique, even when you are faced with the task of 'digging' the ball out of very heavy rough.

Many of the world's leading players, including Hale Irwin, use similar methods for their chips and pitches although not for their long game.

7: Putting

PUTTING successfully is the most elusive aspect of golf because it depends in part on the operation of the subconscious mind. However, the putt is golf's winning stroke and I think it is worthwhile repeating part of the analysis of the matter contained in my previous book.

To be a good competitor you have to be a reasonable putter. The proficient putter will always have a different attitude to the game from the poor putter. After a bad shot it is a challenge to the good putter still to achieve his par. He knows he has a good chance to recover the lost ground if he can place his shot to the green reasonably close to the pin. In contrast, the poor putter usually accepts the loss of a shot and is, of necessity, a defensive player.

Everyone has had days when all the putts go in. The line is easy and judgment of distance is no trouble. The problem is to make these days more frequent. How can this be done?

Firstly, there is the matter of feel. It is perfectly easy to roll a golf ball up to the hole using the hand. You have a very precise feel for what you are doing. The difficulty is to retain as much as possible of this feel once the putter is interposed between hand and ball. Once again, it is a question of pressure at impact.

It might seem that the ball is on the putter for a very short time and that the putting stroke is merely a collision between the clubhead and the ball. This is not so. The putt, like other golf shots, should be the application of force through a distance.

The putter should be swung very slowly with as much pressure as possible behind the shot so that the flexing of the shaft can keep the ball on the blade of the putter for as great a distance as possible. In this way the body has time to transmit to the brain the feel of what is happening and you achieve maximum control.

The swing described earlier in this book enables the fullest possible pressure to be applied to the ball in the full shot and I use exactly the same technique for putting. This is contrary to the practice of most golfers, who usually regard putting as a game within a game and have a putting technique which is vastly different from the technique they used up to the green. In my view, this is another recipe for disaster, no matter what type of full swing you favour.

It is difficult enough to master one method without trying to master two. If you have two separate techniques, there is always a tendency for one to take over from the other, or for one to be working when the other isn't. Bobby Locke was, and still is, one of the world's greatest putters, and he has not lost his skill because his putting stroke is a miniature of the full swing. In contrast, Ben Hogan and Arnold Palmer are just two of the great golfers who lost their touch on the greens because their putting stroke was *not* a miniature of their full swing.

When the putting method is a miniature of the full shot, every putt helps to make the swing more automatic—the method of taking up the stance, of seeing the line, of starting the swing, and the all-important matter of tempo. The need for a sound method in which there is no hint of hitting with the hands is particularly vital when you are putting under pressure, which is an entirely different matter from putting. The hands are weak, highly flexible and the first part of the body to reflect nervousness.

Once you have studied a putt, made a decision on the line and stored enough information in your subconscious to assess the strength of the putt, the real test can be divided into two parts—hitting the ball on line and hitting it at the right pace.

Hitting the ball on the intended line is first a matter of being able to see the line from the ball to the hole when the address position has been taken up. I have used the expression 'the right eye coming up under the left' several times in this book. In putting this is even more essential.

At the address, both eyes should be in the same vertical plane—that is, the right eye below the left. This position can be clarified in your mind by taking up a stance to putt towards a mirror. As you look towards the mirror as if to check the line of the putt, the reflection of both eyes and the balls hould be vertically above one another.

This is probably not necessary for golfers with a strong master eye, but it does help even for them. With most golfers, however, it is possible to see a clear line to the hole only when one eye is above the other in this vertical plane. If they are not, each eye sees a slightly different line.

Hitting the ball an exact distance is a more-involved problem. In the first place, I consider the ball should roll from the moment it is struck. All other golf shots depend on backspin for flighting and control, but in putting the situation is virtually reversed. By rolling the ball, I mean it must not skid by having either backspin or overspin.

It is instinctive for players of billiards or pool to strike the cue ball above the centre so that it rolls from the moment of impact. In scientific terms, they are applying a force through the centre of gyration. The centre of gyration is five-sevenths of the diameter up from the ground. With a golf ball, this is a point about a third of an inch above the centre, which is much higher than you would think.

If you push a drum of oil with your foot, it is very difficult to control it as you have difficulty in applying the force above the centre. However, if you push with the hands well above the centre, the drum rolls quite easily and—as is true of a golf ball—the imperfections of the ground do not affect the direction to the same extent because the drum is rolling.

In putting, it is obviously not possible to strike the top of the ball to make it roll and a normal putter, which has a loft of from three to five degrees, applies a considerable amount of backspin if it is travelling horizontally at the moment of impact. Using a putter with negative loft does not work either because the ball is driven into the ground and bounces.

The only way to make the ball roll from the start of the putt is to hood the club and strike the ball on the upswing. That is, the ball is well forward at the address and the club is dragged through the ball with the hands ahead of the clubhead. This is the method employed by most good putters, and it is noticeable that their putts always seem to be falling short, but never are.

I think the only putter I have seen who really managed to start the ball rolling from the moment he struck it was Bobby Locke. The first putt I ever saw him take was in a practice round in 1949 when he was at the height of his career. He had a 35-yard putt across a sloping green and downhill. He studied the putt from both ends and from the sides, as well as looking into the hole. Then, after two practice swings,

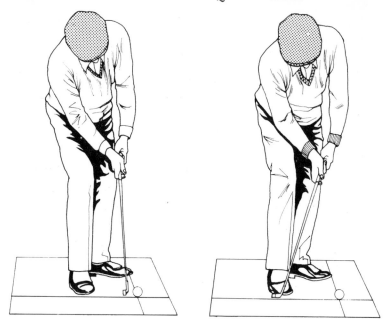

Fig. 29.   Fig. 30.

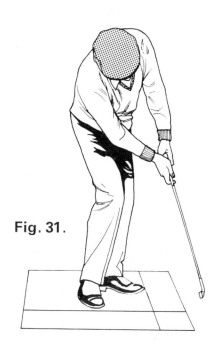

Fig. 31.

he rolled the ball right across the green and slotted it home.

A spectator made the comment: 'You'd have liked that in the tournament,' implying that Bobby was wasting his luck. Bobby raised his hat, put down another ball and holed it at exactly the same speed.

In recent years I have had the privilege of playing a few rounds with him and he was still a great putter. He had a shut stance and hit the ball very much from inside to out with the putter rolling over the ball like a top-spin tennis shot. He would actually draw the ball on a flat green. I do not know of anyone on the tournament circuit today with a reputation as a good putter who can match his perfection of strike.

The putting method I use myself is illustrated in Figs. 29, 30 and 31.

The Address

After studying the putt from both ends and deciding on the line, as well as assessing the speed of the green, I set myself up in the address position shown in Fig. 29 by adopting the same routine as for the full shot.

- My left thumb is around the shaft and the fore-finger of the left hand overlaps the little finger of the right.
- I approach the putt from behind.
- I pick a spot about two feet ahead of the ball and on the line of the putt, and place the putter behind the ball at right angles to this line.
- I set the feet as shown, with the ball off my left toe.
- My head faces the spot about two feet ahead

of the ball, and by turning the head, with the right eye under the left eye, I can check the line to the hole.

In fact, with the head facing the spot two feet ahead of the ball, you can see the hole out of the corner of your eye even when looking at the ball. This is important. One of the difficulties with putting, as in the full shot, is that you are inclined to anticipate the movement and look up just before impact. It is not the looking up that destroys the shot, but the fact that the body has come round with the head.

If you have the head in such a position at the address that you can see the putter, the in-focus ball and the out-of-focus hole, your eye can follow this line without affecting the mechanics of the swing and the inclination to look up before contact is greatly reduced.

The Putt

The actual stroke is a miniature of my full shots. I . . .

- Brace the right leg.
- Swing the clubhead back, pushing the right hand under the left.

The movement (Fig. 30) is quite small, but very easy to control. Again, as with the full shot, the impression is that I am taking the club back so that I can drag the clubhead through the ball. This means that the legs brace against the takeaway and so move just slightly towards the hole. The drag-through means the hands are passive, and, although the club is held quite firmly, the wrists are relaxed. At the actual putt . . .

- There is a good angle between the club and arms.
- The clubhead is hooded as it makes contact very much on the upswing (Fig. 31).
- The right eye follows the putt, coming up under the left.

This gives the impression of bowling the ball up to the hole with a good feel for length.

The mental attitude is also very important. The decision on the line should be taken deliberately, but not too slowly; the set-up should be made carefully; and, when addressing the ball, you should have the attitude that you are enjoying the shot and are determined to make a success of it.

My technique is meant to solve the main problems of putting—to hit the ball on line, to have touch, and to be able to hole the important pressure putts.

8: The Reflex Swing and You

THE golfer who has read this book and feels that what I have said makes sense is bound to have two questions uppermost in his mind.

Will this swing improve my game?

Can I build it in by easy stages?

The answer to both questions is yes.

The swing I have outlined is not by any means revolutionary. It merely carries present development trends to their logical conclusion.

John H. Taylor, as I pointed out in one of the early chapters of this book, had a stance which was 45 degrees open. He was recognised as the greatest golfer of all time when he won the British Open in 1894 and 1895. However, in 1896 he tied with the young Harry Vardon, who proceeded to win the play-off. It is interesting to note that Vardon was at that time considered highly unorthodox because he not only used shorter and lighter clubs but *stood square*. His phenomenal success from that point on ensured that the world copied him. I don't think it is fanciful to say that, in 1896, golf was faced by a fork in the road and chose the wrong path. At the same time, there has always been an inclination to return to the method which John H. Taylor pioneered.

Each generation of golfers has a stance which is slightly more open, particularly in the short game, than the stance of the previous generation. They have found, without necessarily knowing why, that it makes it easier for them to hit the ball. I hope I have been able to give an adequate explanation—that an open stance improves posture, the foundation of the swing, and prevents the centrifugal force of the club-head from pulling you up off the ball.

The most important point is the position of the right elbow. Any swing is improved by getting the right elbow well across the body at the address. With the right elbow and the hands well forward, it is possible to keep the clubhead travelling towards the target much longer because the wrists roll over much later (although I would prefer that they did not roll over at all).

Adopting my head position with the right eye looking underneath will also give a better posture and render it much easier to make contact with the ball. Having the hands low will aid the short game. Making sure the left wrist is bowed, not cupped, at the top of the swing should bring immediate results. So will swinging with passive hands. Finally, the feeling of pushing the club away from you and dragging it through the ball for all shots makes golf a much easier game.

Nobody should expect miracles, however. To develop a sound technique, whether for playing the piano, throwing the javelin or hitting a golf ball, requires daily practice over years. Everyone knows that to reach the top as a pianist means hours of work daily for a decade or more although the actual movements with the fingers are quite simple movements.

Similarly, should you decide to write left-handed when you are right-handed by instinct, you would know how to hold the pen and what to do with it, but it would take months, or even years, of dedicated practice to become fluent.

Most golfers tend to believe they could become good almost overnight if only they could find the secret, or if only they had the time to play every day for a few months. This is an illusion. Muscle-memorising a technique is a long process, which, in golf, is not made any easier by the current lack of agreement about the 'correct' way of playing the game. In fact, practice for most golfers today means experimenting with their grip, stance, takeaway and so on in an endeavour to recapture a feeling they once experienced when they hit 'the perfect shot'.

Practice must be a habit. It must be pleasant, and it must be accessible and available whenever there is a spare moment. Mastering any technique is a matter of going through the movements over and over again, first in slow motion and at minimum effort, then gradually increasing the power while still being meticulous about each element of the swing. To those who do not fully appreciate the extent of the problem, the slow progress is frustrating, and it is only the very determined who do not give up.

Anyone who is serious about his golf swing should set up a place to swing a club or hit balls into a net; a place to chip balls into a chair; and a carpet area to practice putting. The most essential of these three areas is a place to chip. Practicing chipping is the best method of developing a technique because the small amount of effort in the shot is easier to control and a great number of shots can be hit in quite a short time. Development of a good chipping technique can be the basis of a good swing.

You can spend a lifetime improving your swing. Indeed, most professionals do. To obtain the most from your golf you should practice 20 to 30 minutes each day so that, over the years, your swing will develop and your game improve. The habit of daily practice is an essential part of maintaining an enthusiasm for the game.

It might be argued that it is not in the nature of the average golfer to practice daily. However, the argument is believed by my experience with a practice club I developed called the Swingrite, which simulates striking a ball without the disadvantages of actually having a ball there (80 per cent of your concentration goes into making contact with the ball instead of being devoted to developing your swing). Those which come back for servicing have, in most cases, been swung hundreds of times daily over a period of years.

I am certain that, if the average golfer is prepared to set up the areas I have suggested and make the effort to practice daily, using the technique I have outlined, his golf will improve immeasurably over the years. As it is a scientifically sound technique, based on the natural way the body works, it will not cause—and is, in fact, more likely to cure—bad backs. Furthermore, with the legs, the strongest muscles of the body, being used as the source of power, nobody need experience that disastrous loss of distance which causes so many golfers to give up the game as the years roll by.

But don't forget—*keep that right elbow well across* the body. Otherwise you are wasting your time.